16-19 MATHEMATICS

Mathematical structure

The School Mathematics Project

CAMBRIDGE
UNIVERSITY PRESS

Main authors	Chris Belsom
	Stan Dolan
	Paul Roder
	Jeff Searle
Project director	Stan Dolan

The authors would like to give special thanks to Ann White for her help in preparing this book for publication.

The publishers would like to thank the following for supplying photographs:

page 26 - Ann Ronan Picture Library

page 39 - Holt Studios Ltd.

page 75 - Ann Ronan Picture Library

page 92 - Christopher Charlton

Cartoons by Margaret Ackroyd

Published by the Press Syndicate of the University of Cambridge
The Pitt Building, Trumpington Street, Cambridge CB2 1RP
40 West 20th Street, New York, NY 10011–4211, USA
10 Stamford Road, Oakleigh, Melbourne 3166, Australia

© Cambridge University Press 1991

First published 1991
Third printing 1994

Produced by 16-19 Mathematics, Southampton

Printed in Great Britain
by Scotprint Ltd, Musselburgh

ISBN 0 521 42650 2

Contents

1 Binary operations

1.1 Structure

The **structure** of a building refers to the way it is made or put together as distinct from its superficial decorations.

Two houses with the same structure can therefore look very different.

Analogously, mathematicians try to ignore superficial aspects of objects they are studying and concentrate on the underlying **mathematical structure**. This unit of the 16-19 course concentrates on helping you to discover precisely what is meant by structure and why mathematicians regard such a study as important.

Many games have an underlying structure which you can use to help improve your play.

Noughts and crosses, for example:

There are essentially only two replies for O, one draws and the other loses.

> **Explain the above statement for the game of 'noughts and crosses'.**

The game of 'fifteen-up' is likely to be new to you.

In the game of 'fifteen-up', two players take it in turns to choose counters from a set of 9 labelled with the digits 1 to 9.

The winner is the first person whose set of counters contains 3 which add up to 15
e.g. ①, ⑤, ⑨.

 | **Play a number of games of 'fifteen-up'. Try to develop a strategy for playing the game.**

1

1.2   Notation for transformations

The *Problem solving* unit of 16-19 Mathematics material contains the following example:

Three tumblers are placed upside down on a table.

You take any pair and turn them over, and continue doing this, a pair at a time, in an effort to finish with all three right way up. Invent a simple notation to explain why this is not possible.

> **What notation helps to explain the impossibility?**

The solutions to *Problem solving* gave a notation for various **positions of tumblers.** Another method is to have a notation for the various types of **turn.**

For example:

L represents turning over the two tumblers on the left;
R represents turning over the two tumblers on the right.

The use of notation for transformations rather than positions is especially important in this unit because transformations can be **combined.**

> **If L ∘ R means *perform R and then L*, describe the transformation L ∘ R. Similarly, describe L ∘ L, R ∘ R and R ∘ L.**
>
> **Denoting L ∘ R by O and L ∘ L by N, copy and complete the table below.**

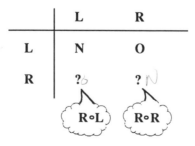

	L	R
L	N	O
R	?o	?N

R∘L   R∘R

The entries in a combination table, in this case **L**, **R**, **N** and **O**, are usually called the **elements.**

Starting with just the elements **L** and **R**, two new elements, **N** and **O**, have been produced. **N** leaves the tumblers unchanged and is the single transformation which is equivalent to both **L ∘ L** and **R ∘ R**. **O** turns the two outside tumblers over and is the single transformation which is equivalent to both **L ∘ R** and **R ∘ L**.

A table of combinations for **L, R, N** and **O** can be obtained:

	N	L	R	O
N	N	L		O
L		N	O	
R	R			L
O	O			

> **Complete the table.**
>
> **What extra elements have now been obtained?**
>
> **How does this show that the three tumblers *cannot* all be turned right way up?**

The notation given in *Problem solving* was 1 for an upright tumbler and 0 for one which is upside down. This led to a simple proof that the tumblers could not be all turned upright:

Two tumblers are turned over each time and so the sum is always 0 or 2, never 3, as required.

The new notation leads to the same result.

*Any combination of turns from the original position is equivalent to one of the four turns, **L, R, N** and **O** and therefore cannot turn all the tumblers upright.*

The first notation is probably better for solving this particular problem. However, the second notation has led to a new idea of **combining** transformations, an idea which will prove very useful in our study of **structure.**

> **For any two transformations L and R,**
>
> **L ∘ R means *perform R and then L*.**

3

Example 1

Find the combination table for the rotations and reflections which **fix** a rectangle i.e. leave it occupying its original position. Compare this table with the combination table for turning the tumblers.

Solution

The rectangle is fixed by
l: a reflection in the *x*-axis;
m: a reflection in the *y*-axis;
r: a rotation of 180° about *O*
(a half turn);
I: the identity transformation,
not moving the rectangle at all!

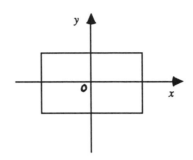

> Find l∘ l, m∘ m, r∘ r and l∘ m.

The combination tables for the rectangle and the tumblers are:

∘	I	l	m	r
I	I	l	m	r
l	l	I	r	m
m	m	r	I	l
r	r	m	l	I

∘	N	L	R	O
N	N	L	R	O
L	L	N	O	R
R	R	O	N	L
O	O	R	L	N

The tables are the same apart from the symbols used. It is perhaps not surprising that **I** should correspond to **N** - both change nothing at all! It is perhaps more surprising why, say, a reflection should correspond to turning over two tumblers.

> **The result of performing any transformation of the rectangle twice is the identity transformation and similarly for any turn of the tumblers.**
>
> **Write down at least one other result which must hold for both the rectangle and the tumblers.**

4

1.3   Isomorphic structures

When tackling the opening game of 'fifteen-up' you may have been able to develop a strategy which ensured that you never lost. In fact, there is a clever way of seeing that 'fifteen-up' and 'noughts and crosses' are essentially the same game and so a strategy for one can be applied to the other.

The array

6	1	8
7	5	3
2	9	4

enables you to establish the equivalence between the two games. Choosing a 6 is equivalent to moving in the top left corner and similarly for any other move.

> **To convince yourself that this does establish the equivalence of the two games, what must you check now ?**

The word 'isomorphism' is used in mathematics to indicate that two mathematical structures have the same (iso-) form (-morphism). For the last two games this isomorphism indicates that there is a complete correspondence between all the moves.

Choose a 6   ↔   go in the top left corner
Choose a 5   ↔   go in the central square
etc.

There must, of course, be more that just this correspondence. For the two structures to be the same, a winning combination in one must be equivalent to a winning combination in the other. For example

$7 + 5 + 3$ ↔

You have seen that the game of 'fifteen-up' has the same structure as 'noughts and crosses' i.e. the two games are **isomorphic** despite having very different appearance. If you know how to play 'noughts and crosses' well, then you can employ the same strategy to 'fifteen-up'.

> **Mathematicians study structure because if they can solve a problem in one situation then the result holds in all isomorphic structures.**

You have also seen another example of isomorphic structures. In Section 1.2, the combination tables for the rectangle and tumblers were:

	I	l	m	r
I	I	l	m	r
l	l	I	r	m
m	m	r	I	l
r	r	m	l	I

	N	L	R	O
N	N	L	R	O
L	L	N	O	R
R	R	O	N	L
O	O	R	L	N

Again, there is a correspondence between the elements

$$I \leftrightarrow N$$
$$l \leftrightarrow L$$
$$m \leftrightarrow R$$
$$r \leftrightarrow O$$

such that **combinations** also correspond e.g.

$$l \leftrightarrow L, \ m \leftrightarrow R \text{ and } l \circ m \leftrightarrow L \circ R$$
$$l \leftrightarrow L, \ r \leftrightarrow O \text{ and } l \circ r \leftrightarrow L \circ O$$

> **How can you tell from the combination table that all combinations correspond appropriately?**

Example 2

Which of the following three combination tables are for isomorphic structures? Justify your answer.

(a)

	0	1	2
0	0	1	2
1	1	2	0
2	2	0	1

(b)

	a	b	c
a	c	a	b
b	a	b	c
c	b	c	a

(c)

	X	Y	Z
X	Y	X	Z
Y	Z	Y	X
Z	X	Z	Y

Solution

Just one of the many ways of seeing that (c) cannot be isomorphic to either of the other two tables is to note that

$$X \ Y \neq Y \ X$$

whereas the order in which elements are combined does not matter in (a) or (b).

Transforming $0 \to \mathbf{b}$, $1 \to \mathbf{a}$, $2 \to \mathbf{c}$ in (a) gives:

	b	a	c
b	b	a	c
a	a	c	b
c	c	b	a

Reordering the rows and columns of this table gives (b):

	a	b	c
a	c	a	b
b	a	b	c
c	b	c	a

and so (a) and (b) **are** isomorphic.

> **Show that $0 \leftrightarrow \mathbf{b}$, $1 \leftrightarrow \mathbf{c}$, $2 \leftrightarrow \mathbf{a}$ also sets up an isomorphism between (a) and (b).**

Exercise 1

1. The following game is from the work of the mathematical psychologist Dienes. Six children are arranged in a ring as shown. They can pass a ball between themselves according to certain rules. The passes allowed are:

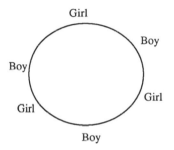

A   A girl passes the ball to the next girl on her right or a boy passes it to the next boy on his left.

B   A girl passes the ball to the next girl on her left or a boy passes it to the next boy on his right.

C   A child passes the ball to the child opposite.

D   A girl passes the ball to the boy on her right or a boy passes it to the girl on his left.

E   A girl passes the ball to the boy on her left or a boy passes it to the girl on his right.

Complete the table where $\mathbf{C} \circ \mathbf{D} = \mathbf{B}$ denotes that the result of performing $\mathbf{D}$ then $\mathbf{C}$ is the same as the result of performing pass $\mathbf{B}$. **I** denotes not passing the ball at all.

∘	I	A	B	C	D	E
I						
A						
B						
C					B	
D						
E						

2. Imagine an equilateral triangle on a fixed plane with lines **l**, **m** and **n** as shown:

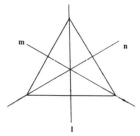

N.B. The lines **l**, **m**, **n**, are fixed in the plane and do not move when the triangle moves.

The triangle is fixed by:

I : the identity transformation.
R : a rotation of 120° (anticlockwise)
S : a rotation of 240°
L : a reflection in line **l**
M : a reflection in line **m**
N : a reflection in line **n**

Complete the combination table

○	I	R	S	L	M	N
I						
R						
S						
L						
M						
N						

3. What do you notice about your tables for questions 1 and 2? What does this imply about Dienes' game and the rotations and reflections which fix an equilateral triangle?

4. List some of the features of the table for the rectangle considered in Section 1.2.

5. List some of the features of the table for the equilateral triangle in question 2.

1.4   Elements and operations

You have seen how two elements can be combined according to some defined operation. For example, in the tumblers problem you saw that **L** followed by move **R** had the same effect as performing the single move O. A convenient notation for writing this down symbolically is

$$\mathbf{R} \circ \mathbf{L} = \mathbf{O}$$

The symbol ○ represent the operation and the symbol = has its usual meaning of **is the same as**. In this example the moves symbolised by **L** and **R** are the elements.

There are many other examples of elements and operations, some of which you are already very familiar with.

If you let the elements be whole numbers and consider the operations of addition and division, the beginnings of the combination tables are as shown below:

addition

+	1	2	3	4	...
1	2	3	4	5	...
2	3	4	5	6	...
3	4	5	6	7	...
4	5	6	7	8	...
.	.	.	.	.	
.	.	.	.	.	

division

÷	1	2	3	4	...
1	1	$\frac{1}{2}$	$\frac{1}{3}$	$\frac{1}{4}$	...
2	2	1	$\frac{2}{3}$	$\frac{1}{2}$	...
3	3	$\frac{3}{2}$	1	$\frac{3}{4}$	...
4	4	2	$\frac{4}{3}$	1	...
.	.	.	.	.	
.	.	.	.	.	

> (a)   **Why is it impossible to write down the whole combination table?**
>
> (b)   **State some of the features of each of the two tables above.**

There are many other operations on whole numbers which could be considered. Apart from the obvious ones of multiplication and subtraction, there are such operations as:

$[a, b]$ is the highest common factor of a and b.
$a \uparrow b$ is a^b
etc.

There are many other types of elements and associated operations in mathematics with which you are also familiar. For example:

functions

elements: functions
operations: addition, subtraction, multiplication, division, combination

$$\text{If } f(x) = 3x \text{ and } g(x) = x + 2, \text{ then:}$$
$$f(x) + g(x) = 3x + x + 2 = 4x + 2$$
$$f(x).g(x) \quad = 3x\,(x + 2) = 3x^2 + 6x$$
$$f\{g(x)\} \quad\quad = 3(x + 2) = 3x + 6$$

vectors

elements: any representation of vectors, e.g. directed line segments
operations: addition, subtraction

$\mathbf{a} + \mathbf{b} = \mathbf{c}$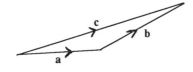

All the types of operation we have considered are called **binary** operations because **two** elements are combined each time.

> The terms *element* and *binary operation* are formal terms used in the study of structure in mathematics.
>
> We can write $a * b = c$
> where a, b and c are the elements and $*$ is the binary operation.

Exercise 2

1. Insert a suitable operation between the two elements on the left of the equals sign to give the element on the right hand side.

   (a) $3 \;\square\; 5 = 8$ (b) $5 \;\square\; ^-3 = 8$

   (c) $3 \;\square\; 4 = 12$ (d) $3 \;\square\; 4 = 81.$

2. Define an operation $*$ to mean *add twice the first number to half the second*.

   For example $2 * 6 = 7$.

   What are the results of the following?

   (a) $3 * 4$ (b) $4 * 3$ (c) $0 * 5$ (d) $4 * 4$

3. Find the result of the following operations on the elements A, B and C, all of which are polynomials.

$$A = 2x - 1 \qquad B = 3x^2 - 2x + 5 \qquad C = x^3 - 4x + 1$$

(a) B – A

(b) B + C

(c) AC

(d) CA

4. If f: $x \rightarrow 2x$ and g:$x \rightarrow x - 1$

express fg in the form fg:$x \rightarrow$

express gf in the form gf:$x \rightarrow$

What are the 'elements' in this question and what is the operation used to combine them?

5. Suppose that rotations of this **triquetra** of 0°, 120° and 240° are denoted by **I**, **P** and **Q** respectively.

Complete the combination table for these rotations.

	I	P	Q
I			
P			
Q			

1.5   Clock or modulo arithmetic

Your familiarity with arithmetic operations probably extends to a special form of arithmetic associated with clocks.

> **Think of conventional clocks and describe why it is sensible to write symbolised statements such as**
>
> (a) $10 + 4 = 2$ (b) $1 - 5 = 8.$

There is an arithmetic associated with a clock face which has only 12 elements. You can obtain some interesting results in algebraic structure from this arithmetic and, unlike usual arithmetic, there is the added bonus of a finite combination table.

> **Clock arithmetic is more formally called modulo arithmetic.**

Conventional clock faces show 12 hours.

Mathematicians take the liberty of inventing and studying any **clock** they like.

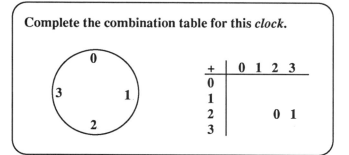

> **Complete the combination table for this *clock*.**
>
> | + | 0 | 1 | 2 | 3 |
> |---|---|---|---|---|
> | 0 | | | | |
> | 1 | | | | |
> | 2 | | | 0 | 1 |
> | 3 | | | | |

The idea of clock arithmetic can be extended to multiplication.

The combination table for combining the elements 1, 2, 3 and 4 under the operation **multiplication modulo 5** is

x	1	2	3	4
1	1	2	3	4
2	2	4	1	3
3	3	1	4	2
4	4	3	2	1

> **Explain some of the entries in the above combination table.**

Exercise 3

1. Write out an addition table for a clock with elements 0, 1, 2, 3, 4 and 5.

2. Write out an addition table under clock rules for the two elements 0 and 1. (This is formally called addition modulo 2.)

3. All positive whole numbers are either odd or even so another way of obtaining a finite combination table for addition is to classify the numbers under these two headings.

   Complete the table

+	E	O
E		
O		

   and comment on the relationship between this table and that from question 2.

4. By rearranging the rows and columns of the combination table for multiplication modulo 5:

x	1	2	3	4
1	1	2	3	4
2	2	4	1	3
3	3	1	4	2
4	4	3	2	1

   demonstrate isomorphism with addition modulo 4 on the elements 0, 1, 2 and 3.

5. Explain why addition modulo 4 on the elements 0, 1, 2 and 3 cannot be isomorphic to the transformations of a rectangle:

	I	l	m	r
I	I	l	m	r
l	l	I	r	m
m	m	r	I	l
r	r	m	l	I

   $m + m \neq 0$

13

1.6   Does the order matter?

In day to day life the order in which activities are carried out is often important. Performing the activities the other way round could produce bizarre results.

In the tumblers problem, you saw that you could write $R \circ L = L \circ R$ as both these expressions were equivalent to the single symbol O.

> **For all possible pairs of moves in the tumblers problem show that the order of the moves does not matter.**
>
> **Why can you be certain that this is also true of the transformations of a rectangle?**

Consider again the transformations of an equilateral triangle.

Let R and S be rotations through 120° and 240° respectively and let L, M and N be reflections in the lines l, m and n respectively.

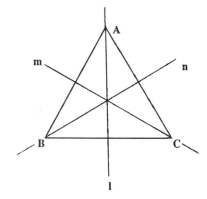

Clearly, rotation R followed by S will have the same effect as rotation S followed by R i.e.

$$R \circ S = S \circ R.$$

However, reflection in line l, followed by reflection in line m, would first take vertex C to B and then to A, whereas reflection in line m followed by reflection in line l, would first leave vertex C unaffected and then move it to B.

So $L \circ M \neq M \circ L.$

The combination table for the transformations is

°	I	R	S	L	M	N
I	I	R	S	L	M	N
R	R	S	I	M	N	L
S	S	I	R	N	L	M
L	L	N	M	I	S	R
M	M	L	N	R	I	S
N	N	M	L	S	R	I

> **Use the combination table to say for which pairings of elements *a* and *b***
>
> $$a * b = b * a$$

In ordinary arithmetic, the order of the numbers sometimes matters and sometimes it does not, depending on the operation that combines the two numbers.

For example $3 + 4 = 4 + 3 = 7$ whereas $3 - 4 \neq 4 - 3$

and $3 \times 4 = 4 \times 3 = 12$ whereas $3 \div 4 \neq 4 \div 3$

> **A binary operation * is said to be *commutative* if, for all possible pairs of elements *a* and *b*, $a * b = b * a$.**

A binary operation, by definition, must be between two, and only two, elements. However, the result of combining two elements could then be combined with a third element.

For example, in, ordinary arithmetic we have:

$(3 + 5) + 7 = 8 + 7 = 15$ or $3 + (5 + 7) = 3 + 12 = 15$

$(2 \times 3) \times 5 = 6 \times 5 = 30$ or $2 \times (3 \times 5) = 2 \times 15 = 30$

> **Demonstrate that the same *order does not matter* rule as illustrated above for addition and multiplication does *not* hold for subtraction and division.**

A binary operation * is said to be *associative* if, for all possible triples of elements a, b and c,

$$a * (b * c) = (a * b) * c = a * b * c$$

When an operation is associative we do not need to insert brackets around pairs of elements and can simply write, for example

$$3 + 5 + 7.$$

Exercise 4

1. Let the operation θ be defined by $a \theta b = a^2 b$. Find the value of

   (a) $1 \theta 2$ (b) $2 \theta 1$ (c) $5 \theta 5$ (d) $0 \theta 5$

   (e) $(1 \theta 3) \theta 1$ (f) $1 \theta (3 \theta 1)$ (g) $^-2 \theta 2$ (h) $2\theta^-2$

   (i) $(^-1 \theta 2) \theta 3$ (j) $^-1 \theta (2 \theta 3)$

   Does $a \theta b = b \theta a$ for all a and b?

   Does $(a \theta b) \theta c = a \theta (b \theta c)$ for all a, b and c?

2. Define operation * to be $a * b = 2a + b$ where a and b are real numbers.

   (a) Is operation * commutative?   (b) Is operation * associative?

3. Explain why the operation G, where G in the expression $a G b$ means **take the greater of** is both associative and commutative.

4. For how many pairs of elements a and b must you consider $a * b$ and $b * a$ in order to prove that * is

   (a) commutative   (b) not commutative?

5E. From the combination table for the transformations of the equilateral triangle, select any three elements a, b and c and then find

   (a) $a * (b * c)$ (b) $(a * b) * c$

   You should find that $(a * b) * c = a * (b * c)$. Have you proved that the operation * is associative?

6E. (a) Explain why addition modulo n is commutative.

   (b) Explain why addition modulo n is associative.

After working through this chapter you should :

1. understand the terms:

    binary operation,
    commutativity,
    associativity,
    identity element,
    isomorphism;

2. be familiar with the use of the above terms in structures
    such as :

    ordinary arithmetic,
    modular arithmetic,
    combinations of functions,
    combinations of transformations;

3. appreciate something of the importance of 'structural' ideas
    in mathematics.

1. Draw up combination tables for each of the following.

    (a) Addition modulo 4 on the elements {0, 1, 2, 3}.

    (b) Multiplication modulo 15 on the elements {3, 6, 9, 12}.

    (c) The reflections and rotations that fix a rhombus:

        I is the identity transformation;
        L and **S** are reflections in the long and short diagonals respectively;
        H is the half-turn about the centre.

    Using your tables, explain how an isomorphism can be established between the structures of (a) and (b), but not between (a) and (c) or between (b) and (c).

2. You have studied the reflections and rotations which fix a rectangle. This can be extended to a 3 dimensional cuboid.

    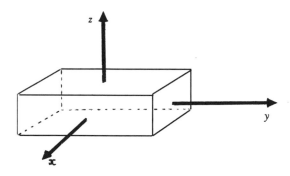

    (a) Considering half-turn rotations about the x, y and z axes together with the identity transformation, draw up a combination table. How is your table related to the combination table for the rectangle?

    (b) Now include reflections in the planes $x = 0$, $y = 0$, $z = 0$. (The yz, xz and xy planes respectively.)

    What is the result of one reflection followed by a different one?

    Extend the combination table so that is now has 7 elements. What do you notice?

    (c) A cuboid is said to be fixed by 8 reflections and rotations. The eighth one is called a **central inversion** and moves each vertex to the diagonally opposite vertex. What combination of half turn and reflection give a central inversion? Complete the combination table for the cuboid.

2 Set algebra

2.1 Set notation

It is often useful to have a diagram to represent information such as the following:

Each child in a certain class can play at most two musical instruments, chosen from cello, flute, piano and violin. The children who play the flute play no other instrument and all children who play the cello also play the violin.

A diagram like the one below is called a Venn diagram after the English mathematician John Venn (1834 - 1923).

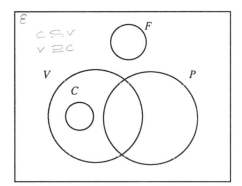

V represents the set of children who play the violin.

P represents the set of children who play the piano.

F represents the set of children who play the flute.

C represents the set of childen who play the cello.

The children in the class fit into one or more 'sets', according to which instruments they play. The diagram makes the relationship between the sets very clear and easy to understand.

> **In the class there are twenty-five children. Eight children play the piano and of these five also play the violin. Eleven children play neither piano nor violin.Use the diagram to determine how many children play the violin.**

In solving the problem you will have had to think very clearly about the way these sets fit together.

The rectangle in the diagram above represents all the children in the class. In any particular context the rectangle represents the set of all things under consideration.

Such a set was originally referred to as the 'universe of discourse' but is now usually called the 'universal set'. It is given a special symbol ' ε ' from the French word *ensemble* for set.

> **The notation used to denote that a set A contains x elements is $n(A) = x$.**

Thus, in the opening example the fact that there are twenty-five children in the class is written as $n(\varepsilon) = 25$.

> **Explain why**
>
> (a) $0 \le n(F) \le 11$ (b) $0 \le n(C) \le 6$

Suppose the set of five children who play both the violin and the piano are:

{Ann, Bernard, Claire, Dennis, Elaine}.

When the individual members of a set are listed, it is conventional to enclose the list in curly brackets as shown above.

Ann is a member of some sets but not of others. The fact that Ann is a member of the set of children who play the piano is written as Ann $\in P$. The fact that she is not a member of the set of children who play the flute is written as Ann $\notin F$.

> **$m \in A$ means that element m is a member of set A.**
>
> **$m \notin B$ means that element m is not a member of set B.**

The Venn diagram on the previous page shows that every child who plays the cello also play the violin. Set C is said to be a **subset** of set V.

> **If every element in set A is also a member of set B, then set A is said to be a subset of set B.**

Note that any set is a subset of itself. The symbol used to denote the relationship 'is a subset of' is similar to the symbol for 'is less than or equal to'.

> **The symbol $\subseteq$ is used to mean 'is a subset of', thus A 'is a subset of' B becomes $A \subseteq B$.**

Just as the 'is less than' symbol has its reverse in the 'is greater than' symbol, so the reverse of the 'is a subset of' symbol denotes the relationship 'includes'.

> **The symbol $\supseteq$ is used to mean 'includes' thus B 'includes' A is written $B \supseteq A$.**

Another symbol often used is a colon ':'. This symbol is simply a shorthand for the phrase 'such that'.

Example 1

Describe the following set in words and list its elements.

$$\{x \in \mathbb{N}: 4 < x < 10\}$$

Solution

'$x \in \mathbb{N}$' means that the elements of the set are members of the set of natural numbers or counting numbers. Thus the set defined above can be described as

'the set of natural numbers which are greater than 4 but less than 10'.

i.e. $\{x \in \mathbb{N} : 4 < x < 10\} = \{5, 6, 7, 8, 9\}$

> If $\mathbb{N}$ is the set of natural numbers and $\mathbb{P}$ is the set of prime numbers, list the elements in
>
> (a) $\{x \in \mathbb{P} : 15 < 2x < 40\}$　　(b) $\{y \in \mathbb{N} : 2y + 3 < 10\}$

In the problem at the start of this chapter the set of five children who play both the violin and the piano was represented by the shaded area in the diagram below. This set is called the **intersection** of sets P and V and is written $P \cap V$. The symbol $\cap$ represents the binary operation of intersection.

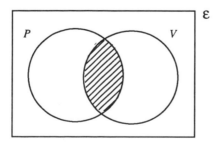

> **P intersection V is written as $P \cap V$.**

Hence $n (P \cap V) = 5$.

If the set of children who play the piano and the set of children who play the violin are combined into one large set, then this new set is represented by the shaded area below and is called the **union** of sets P and V. It is written $P \cup V$ where the symbol $\cup$ represents the binary operation of union.

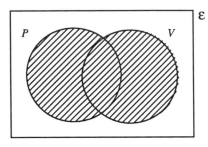

P union V is written as $P \cup V$.

Here $n(P \cup V) = 14$.

If eight children play the piano and there are twenty-five children in the class, then logically it follows that seventeen children in the class do not play the piano. The set of children who do not play the piano is represented by the shaded area below. This set is called the **complement** of set P and is written P'.

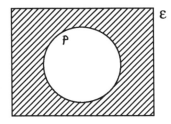

The complement of P is written as P'.

Here $n(P') = 17$.

(a)   Explain why $n(P \cup P') = n(\varepsilon)$.

(b)   Describe the set $P \cap V'$ in words.

(c)   Show $P \cap V'$ on a diagram.

The simplest of sets is the 'empty set'; the set with nothing in it. This set is denoted by the symbol $\varnothing$, a letter taken from the Scandinavian alphabet. $\varnothing$ is the complement of the universal set.

Exercise 1

1. For any set S, simplify:

    (a) $S \cap S'$ (b) $S \cup S'$ (c) $(S')'$ (d) $\varnothing'$

2. Girls at the local secondary school have very little choice in what they can wear as school uniform. They may wear either a dark blue jumper or blue blazer, and either dark grey trousers or dark grey skirt. In the summer, pupils do not necessarily wear either a jumper or blazer. On a school outing during the summer term, all the girls in the third year came in uniform. 15 wore a blazer, 35 wore a jumper and 10 wore trousers. Of those wearing trousers, 3 wore jumpers and 1 wore a blazer. No girl wore both a jumper and a blazer and of those who wore neither a jumper nor a blazer, only 14 wore a skirt.

    (a) Illustrate this on a Venn diagram.

    (b) Find the total number of third year girls on the school outing.

3. In a school of 405 pupils, a survey on sporting activities shows that 251 pupils play tennis, 157 play hockey and 111 play softball. There are 45 pupils who play both tennis and hockey, 60 who play hockey and softball and 39 who play tennis and softball. What conclusions may be drawn about the number of pupils who participate in all three sports?

4. Suppose this Venn digram represents a set of equally likely events.

    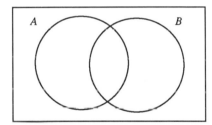

    The notation $P(A)$ represents the probability of an event called A occurring. Using

    $$P(A) = \frac{n(A)}{n(\varepsilon)}, \quad P(A \text{ or } B) = \frac{n(A \cup B)}{n(\varepsilon)} \quad \text{and} \quad P(A \text{ and } B) = \frac{n(A \cap B)}{n(\varepsilon)},$$

    explain why $P(A \text{ or } B) = P(A) + P(B) - P(A \text{ and } B)$.

5. Which of the following are identities? (True for all sets).

    (a) $A \cap A = A$ (b) $A \cap \varnothing = A$ (c) $A \cap \varepsilon = A$

    (d) $A \cap B = B \cap A$ (e) $A \cup \varnothing = A$ (f) $A \cup A = A$

    (g) $A \cup \varepsilon = A$ (h) $A \cup B = B \cup A$

2.2   Boolean algebra

The English mathematician George Boole (1810-1864) is generally recognised as having invented the structure which enables sets to be manipulated. However, it was somewhat later that the Italian mathematician Giuseppe Peano (1858-1932) invented the symbols which are used today.

You have already seen in the previous section that the binary operations of **union** and **intersection** are commutative.

i.e. $A \cup B = B \cup A$ and $A \cap B = B \cap A$

(a)   Is $A \cap (B \cap C) = (A \cap B) \cap C$?

(b)   Is $A \cup (B \cup C) = (A \cup B) \cup C$?

(c)   **What do your answers to (a) and (b) indicate about the operations of union and intersection?**

Taking the complement of a set is an operation applied to just one set. Such an operation is called a **unary** operation. Set algebra is therefore a structure with two binary operations and one unary operation.

Relationships which are true for all sets are known as identities. Before looking at the identities which were developed by 19th century mathematicians, consider the following questions.

Which of the following are identities?

(a) $(A \cup B)' = A' \cap B'$ (b) $(A \cap B)' = A' \cap B'$

(c) $(A \cap B)' = A' \cup B'$ (d) $(A \cup B)' = A' \cup B'$

How would you convince someone that you are right?

An important property sometimes found in structures which contain two binary operations is the **distributive** property. You can think of it as 'the property of being able to multiply out brackets'. For example, multiplication is distributive over addition for real numbers

i.e. $a \times (b + c) = (a \times b) + (a \times c)$

Is addition distributive over multiplication?

The truth (or otherwise) of an identity can be determined by identifying the 'areas' on a Venn diagram which represent the left-hand side (LHS) and right-hand side (RHS) of the supposed identity. Providing the Venn diagram covers all possible cases, the two expressions are 'identical' if, and only if, the two areas are the same.

Example 2

Is union distributive over intersection:

$$\text{is } A \cup (B \cap C) = (A \cup B) \cap (A \cup C)?$$

Solution

LHS

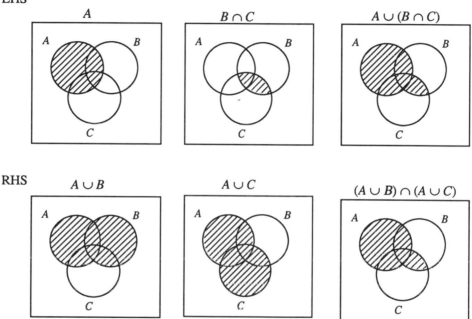

RHS

As the shaded 'area' is the same for both sides of the identity, it is clear that the statement is true.

> **Is intersection distributive over union:**
> is $A \cap (B \cup C) = (A \cap B) \cup (A \cap C)?$

The identities established so far and the names by which they are known are shown below. Collectively they form the basis for the algebraic manipulation of sets. The algebraic structure thus defined has become known as Boolean algebra in honour of George Boole. Augustus de Morgan (1806-1871), an English mathematician and contemporary of George Boole, is credited with discovering relationships between these three operations which have since become known as 'De Morgan's laws'.

Basic laws of Boolean algebra

Idempotent laws

$$A \cup A = A \qquad : \qquad A \cap A = A$$

Identity laws

$$A \cup \varnothing = A \qquad : \qquad A \cap \varepsilon = A$$
$$A \cup \varepsilon = \varepsilon \qquad : \qquad A \cap \varnothing = \varnothing$$

Complement laws

$$A \cup A' = \varepsilon \qquad : \qquad A \cap A' = \varnothing$$
$$\varepsilon' = \varnothing \qquad : \qquad \varnothing' = \varepsilon$$
$$(A')' = A$$

Commutative laws

$$A \cup B = B \cup A \qquad : \qquad A \cap B = B \cap A$$

Associative laws $\quad A \cup (B \cup C) = (A \cup B) \cup C \ : \ A \cap (B \cap C) = (A \cap B) \cap C$

Distributive laws

$$A \cup (B \cap C) = (A \cup B) \cap (A \cup C) \ : \ A \cap (B \cup C) = (A \cap B) \cup (A \cap C)$$

De Morgan's laws $\qquad (A \cup B)' = A' \cap B' \quad : \quad (A \cap B)' = A' \cup B'$

Other laws of Boolean algebra can be proved from those given above. For example, in Exercise 2 you will be asked to derive the following:

Absorption laws $\ A \cup (A \cap B) = A \quad : \quad A \cap (A \cup B) = A$

You will note a symmetry in all of the identities given above . If you exchange the symbols $\cup$ and $\cap$ and the sets ε and $\varnothing$ in any of the above identities, another valid identity is obtained. This is known as the **principle of duality.**

Since the dual of each basic law is also a law, then the dual of any result proved from them is also true. The principle of duality is an important structural idea for Boolean algebra.

26

Example 3

Simplify the expression $(A \cap B')' \cup B$ and hence show that $(A \cup B')' \cap B = A' \cap B$.

Solution

$$
\begin{aligned}
(A \cap B')' &= A' \cup (B')' & \text{de Morgan's law} \\
&= A' \cup B & \text{complement law}
\end{aligned}
$$

$$
\begin{aligned}
\Rightarrow \quad (A \cap B')' \cup B &= (A' \cup B) \cup B \\
&= A' \cup (B \cup B) & \text{associative law} \\
&= A' \cup B & \text{idempotent law}
\end{aligned}
$$

$$
(A \cap B')' \cup B = A' \cup B
$$

$$
\Rightarrow \quad (A \cup B')' \cap B = A' \cap B \qquad \text{principle of duality}
$$

> Since $(A \cup B')' \cap B = A' \cap B$, does it follow that $(A \cup B')' = A'$?

Although the identity in Example 2 could have been established by considering Venn diagrams, the method used illustrates the efficiency with which sets can be manipulated symbolically using the laws of Boolean algebra.

Exercise 2

1. Write down the dual of the following Boolean expressions

    (a) $A \cup (A' \cap B)$ (b) $(A \cap B)' \cup \varepsilon$ (c) $(A' \cup \varnothing) \cap (A \cup \varepsilon)$

2. Draw Venn diagrams to show the following sets

    (a) $A \cup (A \cap B)$ (b) $A \cap (A \cup B)$

3. The identity $A \cup (A \cap B) = A$ and its dual $A \cap (A \cup B) = A$ are called the **Absorption Laws**.

    (a) Use the basic axioms listed on the previous page to prove that
    $A \cup (A \cap B) = A$ (Hint: use the identity law $A = A \cap \varepsilon$.)

    (b) Take the dual of each step used in your answer to part (a) and check that they now form a proof that $A \cap (A \cup B) = A$.

4. Draw Venn diagrams to show the following sets

    (a) $A \cup (B \cap C')$ (b) $A' \cap B' \cap C'$ (c) $(A \cap B)' \cap (A \cup B)$

5. Use the basic axioms of Boolean algebra to simplify

    (a) $(A \cup B') \cap (A \cup B)$ (b) $(A \cap B') \cup (A \cap B)$ (c) $A \cup (A \cup B')'$

2.3   Switching circuits

The usefulness of Boolean algebra is not just that it allows mathematicians to manipulate the logical relationships between sets. Earlier this century it was discovered that the underlying mathematical structure of electronic switching circuits is isomorphic to Boolean algebra and so the study of Boolean algebra is now considered to be of more than purely academic interest.

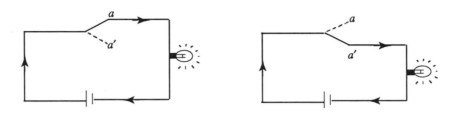

Electrical devices operate when current flows through them. The diagram shows two simple circuits, each with a battery, a lamp and a two-way switch. When the switch is in position a, the first circuit is complete (i.e. closed), the current flows and the lamp lights up. The second circuit is complete when the switch is in position a'. Computer circuits consist of complex arrangements of electronic switches designed to control the flow of current as data is processed. It is beyond the scope of this book to analyse a real computer circuit, but some understanding of the underlying mathematical structure can be gained by looking at simple arrangements of switches.

In many homes a single light is often controlled by 2 two-way switches. A common example of this is where a light can be switched on or off from either the top or the bottom of a stairway.

> **Design a 'stairway' circuit with 2 two-way switches, A and B, and a single light fitting.**

If a circuit has 2 two-way switches, A and B, which can be operated independently, then the switches can be set to any one of four different combinations of position as shown in the tree diagram below.

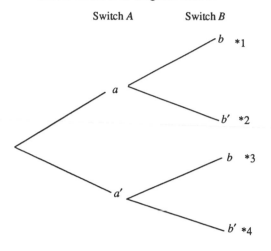

Switch A Switch B

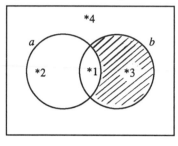

The four different combinations can be represented by the four regions of a Venn diagram.

The region inside the ring labelled a on the Venn diagram represents any combination of settings in which switch A is in position a. The shaded area, $a' \cap b$, represents the particular combination of switch A being set to a' and switch B being set to b. Diagram (i) below shows a circuit in which this particular setting will allow current to flow.

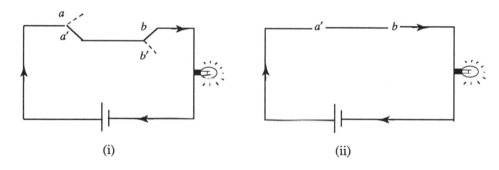

(i)   (ii)

Diagram (ii) shows how such a circuit is conventionally represented. In this diagram switches are represented by letters showing the position of the switch for current to flow. In this circuit the switches are said to be in **series** and are represented by the Boolean expression $a' \cap b$.

The diagram shows two switches in **parallel.** Here current can flow either through a only, or through b only, or through both a and b. So three of the four possible combinations will allow current to flow.

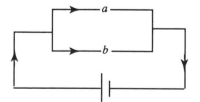

What Boolean expression represents this arrangement?

Example 4

(a)   Write down a Boolean expression to describe this part of a circuit.

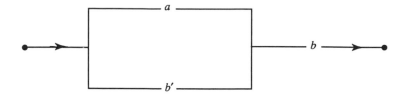

(b)   Simplify the expression and hence construct a simpler equivalent arrangement of switches.

Solution

(a) $(a \cup b') \cap b$

(b)   By the distributive law, this is equivalent to

$(a \cap b) \cup (b' \cap b)$

by the complement law, this is equivalent to

$(a \cap b) \cup \varnothing$

by the identity law, this is equivalent to

$a \cap b$

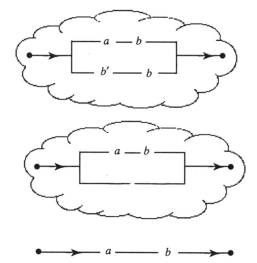

which is the simplest equivalent circuit.

You will notice that switches a and a' both appear in different places in the circuit shown below. This simply means that there are several switches which are linked in such a way that **either** all the switches labelled a are on together **or** all the switches labelled a' are on.

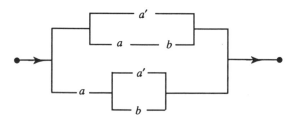

What is the Boolean expression which represents this circuit?

As the underlying mathematical structures of sets and switches are isomorphic, a circuit can be represented as a Boolean expression. The expression can then be simplified using the laws of Boolean algebra and a new circuit constructed which, although simpler, is logically equivalent to, and can replace, the original circuit.

Modern electronic devices such as computers use a different sort of switch called a **logic gate**. The underlying mathematical structure of this, however, is also isomorphic to the algebra of sets and so a branch of mathematics which was once considered pure has now found an important application in the computer industry.

Exercise 3

1. (a) Draw the switching circuit which is represented by the Boolean expression $(a \cup b) \cap (a \cup c)$.

   (b) Use the distributive law to simplify the expression and hence draw a simpler equivalent circuit.

2. The circuit  is equivalent to •——————→•——•——→• .

   Which of the basic axioms of Boolean algebra is illustrated by this example?

3. Draw switching circuits which illustrate the Boolean laws of absorption.

4. Use Boolean algebra to show that these two circuits are equivalent:

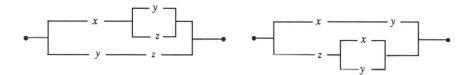

5E. Use the laws of Boolean algebra to show that the circuit

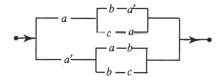

can be simplified to

2.4   Sets of numbers

'God created the integers, all the rest is the work of man'

Leopold Kronecker

Quantities such as the number of eggs in a nest or the number of cars in a car park can be described precisely using numbers.

However, the length of the line shown below presents some problems.

_____

> **Why is it not possible to measure the length of the line precisely?**

For centuries Mathematicians have faced the problem of being unable to quantify with absolute precision, in terms of natural numbers, such things as the length of a line. There is, however, no disputing that the length of the line is a 'real' quantity.

Numbers used to quantify such things as the number of eggs in a nest or the length of a line are called **real numbers.** Real numbers fall into two categories, **rational numbers** and **irrational numbers.**

Rational numbers are numbers which can be described as the ratio of two integers, for example,

$$\frac{5}{8}, \quad \frac{7}{3}, \quad \frac{5}{1}, \quad \frac{-27}{13}, \quad \frac{22}{7}, \text{ etc} \ldots$$

> **Is 3.14 a rational number? Is $0.\dot{1}$ rational?**

Irrational numbers are numbers which cannot be described as the ratio of two integers, for example,

$$\sqrt{2}, \quad \sqrt{3}, \quad \sqrt[3]{7}, \pi, \text{ etc} \ldots$$

The decimal expansions of irrational numbers neither recur nor terminate.

Special symbols are conventionally used for the different categories of number:

> $\mathbb{Q}$ **is the set of rational numbers.**
>
> $\mathbb{Z}$ **is the set of integers.**
>
> $\mathbb{N}$ **is the set of natural numbers.**
>
> $\mathbb{R}$ **is the set of real numbers.**

> **(a) Draw a Venn diagram to show the relationship between these sets.**
>
> **(b) Use set notation to describe the set of rational numbers in terms of $\mathbb{Q}$ and $\mathbb{R}$.**

In 1884, the mathematician Gottlob Frege (1848-1925) published his *Foundations of Arithmetic* in which he attempted formally to define natural numbers in terms of sets. By his definition, the number five, for example, is defined by the set of all collections (sets) of five objects. Five goats, five stones, five children etc..., all share the same property of 'fiveness'.

In 1902, just as Frege was about to publish a second volume in which arithmetic was reconstructed on the foundation of set theory, he received a letter from the young mathematician, Bertrand Russell (1872-1970). Russell pointed out a paradox inherent in the concept of 'a set of all sets' which questioned the basis of Frege's work. This famous paradox has since become known as 'Russell's Paradox'.

Russell pointed out that there are sets which contain themselves as an element, for example 'the set of all sets that have more than five elements'. These sets are known as $\mathfrak{R}$ sets after Russell. Sets which do not contain themselves are known as 'non-$\mathfrak{R}$' sets. For example, the set {1, 2, 3, 4} does not contain itself and is therefore a non-$\mathfrak{R}$ set.

> **Set M is defined as 'the set of all non-$\mathfrak{R}$ sets'.**
> **Is M an $\mathfrak{R}$ set or is it a non-$\mathfrak{R}$ set?**

Russell went on to find a reformulation of set theory which avoided such paradoxes and, together with the mathematician Alfred North Whitehead (1861-1947), he published a major work titled *Principia Mathematica*. The reformulation was so complicated that, in later years, Russell felt that he had failed in his quest to demonstrate that mathematics is nothing but logic.

2.5 Infinity

In the last section you considered sets, such as the set of natural numbers, which contained infinitely many elements. There is a sense in which you can 'count' the elements of **some** infinite sets:

> **A set is said to be countable if you can order the elements in the set according to some rule so that they can be paired off with natural numbers.**

For example, the set of letters needed to write the word 'mathematics' can be ordered alphabetically as

$$\{a, c, e, h, i, m, s, t\},$$

or they can be ordered according to their occurrence in the word itself

$$\{m, a, t, h, e, i, c, s\}.$$

Either way, the elements in the set can be counted by pairing off elements in the set with elements in the set of natural numbers.

$$\mathbb{N} = \{1, 2, 3, 4, 5, 6, 7, 8, 9, \ldots\}$$
$$| \ | \ | \ | \ | \ | \ | \ |$$
$$A = \{m, a, t, h, e, i, c, s\}$$

Thus the number of elements in the set is 8. The number eight is said to be the **cardinal** of the set.

Although the idea of counting the number of elements in a set is very easy to understand, it does produce some interesting paradoxes. Galileo (1564-1642) pointed out the following example.

If you compare the set of natural numbers with the set of square numbers

$$\mathbb{N} = \{1, 2, 3, 4, 5, 6, 7, \ldots\}$$
$$| \ | \ | \ | \ | \ | \ |$$
$$S = \{1, 4, 9, 16, 25, 36, 49, \ldots\}$$

you see that every number has a square, so there must be as many square numbers as there are natural numbers. But many natural numbers are **not** square numbers, for example 2, 3, 5, 6, ... , so there must be 'more' natural numbers than square numbers!

Cantor assigned the symbol $\aleph_0$ (aleph–nought) to the cardinality of the natural numbers. The set of square numbers can be put in one-to-one correspondence with the set of natural numbers and so also has cardinality $\aleph_0$.

The integers, $\mathbb{Z} = \{\ldots, -2, -1, 0, 1, 2, \ldots\}$ can be ordered and paired off with the natural numbers as shown:

$$\mathbb{Z} = \{0, \quad 1, -1, \quad 2, -2, \quad 3, -3, \ldots\}$$
$$| \quad | \quad | \quad | \quad | \quad | \quad |$$
$$\mathbb{N} = \{1, \quad 2, \quad 3, \quad 4, \quad 5, \quad 6, \quad 7, \ldots\}$$

Note that **every** integer is included in this pairing:

- if n is +ve, then n is paired with $2n$.
- if n is –ve, then n is paired with $1 - 2n$.

$\mathbb{Z}$ therefore has cardinality $\aleph_0$.

(a)   **If you combine a set of numbers with $\aleph_0$ members with another set of numbers with $\aleph_0$ members, how many members will the new set have?**

(b)   **What does this suggest about the result of $\aleph_0 + \aleph_0$?**

The German mathematician Georg Cantor (1845-1918) first demonstrated that the set of rational numbers is countable. He showed that there is a way of listing **all** the fractions so that they can be counted **leaving none out**. The diagram below illustrates his method:

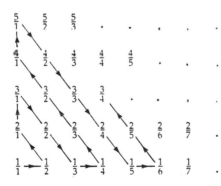

Cantor realised that trying to order fractions according to size was impossible. His method groups together fractions in which the sum of the numerator and denominator is 2, 3, 4, 5, 6, etc..., and then orders the fractions within each group according to the size of the numerator.

Can you be sure that all possible fractions will be included?

Would $\frac{49}{313}$ or $\frac{3594}{13}$ be included, for example?

In addition to proving that the set of rational numbers is countable, Cantor proved that the set of real numbers is **not** countable. He did this by what has become known as his diagonal proof. Cantor's proof is as follows:

Suppose someone claimed that they **had** found a way of listing **all** the real numbers between 0 and 1:

$$0.\cancel{4}\,6\,0\,9\,7\,2\,\ldots$$
$$0.0\,\cancel{0}\,3\,8\,5\,0\,\ldots$$
$$0.5\,2\,\cancel{9}\,9\,9\,5\,\ldots$$
$$0.3\,0\,0\,\cancel{0}\,0\,0\,\ldots$$
$$0.1\,2\,4\,2\,\cancel{9}\,6\,\ldots$$
$$\cdot\;\;\cdot\;\;\cdot\;\;\cdot\;\;\cdot\;\;\cdot\;\;\cdot$$

If you consider the sequence of digits on the diagonal

$$0.4\,0\,9\,0\,9\,\ldots$$

and change every digit after the decimal point, using the rule

$$0 \to 1,\; 1 \to 2,\ldots\ldots,\; 8 \to 9,\; 9 \to 0,$$

you obtain the number

$$0.5\,1\,0\,1\,0\,\ldots$$

This cannot be the 1st number because its 1st digit is different; it cannot be the 2nd number because the 2nd digit is different; it cannot be the 3rd number because the 3rd digit is different; etc... and so it **must** be a new number not included in the list. It is therefore not possible to make a complete list and without such a list you cannot pair off the real numbers with the counting numbers. [In a more detailed proof, care has to be taken because some numbers have two different decimal representations, for example $0.5\dot{0} = 0.4\dot{9}$.]

Cantor reached the conclusion that there are two different kinds of infinity, the countable infinity of the set of natural numbers, $\aleph_0$, and the much bigger infinity of the numbers on a line segment. This latter infinity is not countable and is known as the infinity of the continuum.

The implication of Cantor's work is that between any two irrational numbers there is a rational, yet there are 'more' irrational numbers than there are rationals. Cantor's work was not generally accepted by other mathematicians of the time and his theories came under attack as being 'repugnant to common sense'. These attacks depressed Cantor and in 1918 he died in a mental institution after suffering a series of nervous break-downs. It is only now that Cantor's genius is properly recognised.

After working through this chapter you should:

1. be able to use set notation for:
   - membership of a set $a \in A$
   - subsets $A \subseteq B$
   - complements A'
   - the universal set ε
   - the empty set $\varnothing$
   - union $A \cup B$
   - intersection $A \cap B$
   - cardinality $n(A)$

2. know how to use Venn diagrams to illustrate relationships between sets;

3. appreciate that Boolean algebra forms a structure underlying both that of sets and of switching circuits;

4. appreciate the importance of the principle of duality;

5. be able to prove set algebra results using the laws of Boolean algebra;

6. understand how to represent switching circuits by Boolean expressions and hence how to simplify switching circuits;

7. appreciate that $\mathbb{Q}$ has cardinality $\aleph_0$ but that $\mathbb{R}$ is not countable.

Tutorial sheet

1. Some switching circuits are controlled by 'relay switches'. A relay switch is simply several switches linked mechanically so that all the switches in the relay are either simultaneously 'up' or simultaneously 'down'.

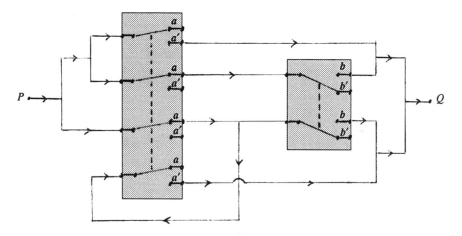

(a) Write down the Boolean expression which represents this circuit.

(b) Use the basic axioms of Boolean algebra to simplify the expression.

(c) Draw a relay switching circuit (similar to the one shown above) to represent your simplified circuit.

2. In the diagram shown below, C is the centre of a semi-circle, S, and L is an infinite line.

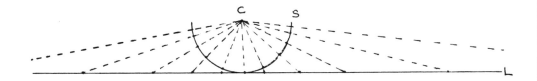

The diagram shows that every point on the line can be paired up with a point on the semi-circle.

'Therefore there are as many points in a finite interval as there are in an inifinite interval'.

Do you agree with this statement? Carefully justify your answer.

3 Group theory

3.1 Symmetry

You will have already come across many examples of 'symmetry'. Some different types of symmetry in nature, mathematics and philosophy, are illustrated below.

Symmetry has often been seen to be connected with beauty, harmony and perfection in nature.

The mathematical idea of symmetry includes more than geometrical transformations.

$$x^4 + 2x^3 + 5x^2 + 2x + 1$$

The Chinese *Diagram of the Supreme Ultimate* uses symmetry to symbolise the dynamic interplay between opposing forces.

> With reference to the above examples, decide what it means to say that something exhibits 'symmetry'. Can you find a general definition which applies to all three of the above examples?

In general, the idea of **symmetry** is connected with the idea of a **transformation.** This does **not** need to be a geometrical transformation such as a reflection or a rotation. In the first examples of symmetry in this section, the transformations included interchanging black and white and replacing x^a by x^{4-a}. When an object is unchanged by a transformation, we refer to **symmetry.**

One of the initial symmetry examples was taken from Taoist philosophy. Symmetry similarly played an important role in Greek philosophy. For example, Plato believed that the atoms of the four elements of earth, fire, air and water had the shapes of the regular solids.

Nowadays, particle physicists apply mathematical ideas of groups of symmetries to the analysis of the fundamental nature of the universe. Although concepts of quantum mechanics and relativity are beyond the scope of this unit, the following example illustrates the way symmetry ideas can be related to other areas of physics.

Consider a head-on collision between two objects of equal mass:

Someone travelling with speed $\frac{u}{2}$ in the same direction as the initial direction of motion, would observe the collision as shown below:

> **Without using any laws of mechanics, explain why you would expect y to equal x. Explain why $v = \frac{u}{2} - x$ and $w = y + \frac{u}{2}$ and hence find $mv + mw$. State what law your reasoning has 'discovered'.**

3.2   Transformations

Some scoreboards and advertising boards consist of an array of squares. Messages and pictures can be formed by flipping squares between black and white.

For ease of wiring, it is suggested that such a board should be set up so that **all** the squares in a given row or column have to be flipped over at the same time. Throughout this section it is assumed that such a wiring has been adopted.

> **For the 4 x 5 board shown below:**
>
> **find which row and column flips can be used to transform pattern A into pattern B;**
>
> **find which can be used to transform B into A;**
>
> **think of a notation that would help you to describe your transformations.**

A.
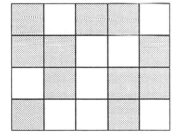

B.
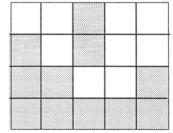

Starting from a blank 4 x 5 board, can you form pattern A?

Starting from a blank _m_ x _n_ board, what patterns can be formed?

Justify your answers.

3.3   Symmetry groups

You have seen that the idea of symmetry is connected with that of a transformation which leaves an object unchanged. Such transformations arc called the **symmetries** of the object. For example, you have already met the symmetries of an equilateral triangle.

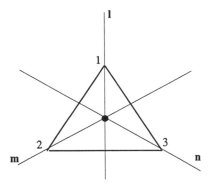

N.B. The axes are fixed in the plane and do not move when the triangle moves.

The triangle has a number of symmetries. It is fixed by

A clockwise rotation of 120° : **R**
A reflection in line **l**   : **L**
A reflection in line **m**   : **M**

> **Complete the above list of symmetries.**

It is quite easy to discover how many symmetries a shape has by the following type of argument:

Choose a vertex of the triangle. Any symmetry takes this vertex into one of three possible vertices. For each choice there are exactly two ways of fixing the triangle and so there are 3 x 2 = 6 symmetries.

If you only listed 5 symmetries above, then it is most likely that you omitted the **identity** transformation which leaves the triangle unchanged!

In your list of transformations you should have included a clockwise rotation of 240° (or, equivalently, an anticlockwise rotation of 120°). Since this rotation is the same as **R** after **R**, it is convenient to denotes this by R^2.

> **What symmetry would R^3 represent?**

You are familiar with the idea of combining transformations by performing one after the other. A symmetry group is the set of symmetries of an object together with the binary operation of combining the transformation.

You have seen that combining symmetries is not always a commutative operation.

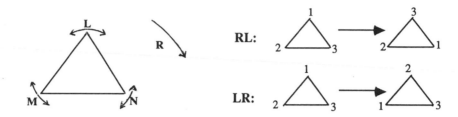

> **If R and S are two symmetries of a shape, then RS is *not* in general equal to SR.**

However, the combination of symmetries does possess some 'common-sense' properties. For example, if **R, S** and **T** are three symmetries of a shape then

        (RS)T means **RS** after **T**

and

        RS means **R** after **S**.

Therefore

        (RS)T means **R** after **S** after **T**.

> **What does R(ST) mean?**

It should be clear that the binary operation of combining symmetries is, by its very nature, **associative**.

> **If R, S and T are three symmetries of a shape, then**
>
> **(RS)T = R(ST)**

Some other properties of symmetry groups are studied on Tasksheet 1.

TASKSHEET 1 - *Group tables*

Closure

If **R** and **S** are two symmetries of a shape, then each individually leaves the shape 'unchanged'. **R** after **S** must also leave the shape unchanged and so **RS** is itself a symmetry.

> **If R and S are two symmetries of a shape, then so is RS.**
>
> **The symmetries of a shape are closed under the binary operation of combining symmetries.**

Closure can be easily seen from the combination table.

	a	b	c
a	•	•	•
b	•	•	•
c	•	•	•

Each element in the body of the table must be a, b or c.

Identity element

The identity transformation, **I**, leaves a shape totally unchanged and so:

> **All symmetry groups possess an identity element I such that, for any other symmetry, R,**
>
> **RI = IR = R.**

From a combination table, the identity transformation can be spotted by its property of not altering the original row and column.

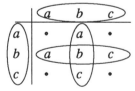

b is the identity element.

44

Inverses

Suppose that **R** is a symmetry of a shape which has identity transformation **I**. If **R** takes point a to point b, then the inverse symmetry, **R**$^{-1}$, takes point b to point a. Then

$$\mathbf{R^{-1}R}: a \rightarrow b \rightarrow a.$$

R^{-1}**R** therefore fixes **all** points of the shape and so **R**$^{-1}$**R** = **I**.
Similarly,

$$\mathbf{RR^{-1}}: b \rightarrow a \rightarrow b$$

Therefore **RR**$^{-1}$ also fixes **all** points and **RR**$^{-1}$ = **I**.

> **For any symmetry R of a shape, there is an inverse symmetry, R^{-1}, such that**
>
> $$\mathbf{RR^{-1} = R^{-1}R = I.}$$

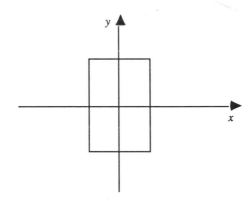

a is self-inverse
b and c are inverses of each other.

Exercise 1

1.

How many symmetries does a rectangle possess? List them all and work out all possible products. What do you notice?

2. How many symmetries does a square possess? Find them all. Show that the combination of these symmetries is not commutative.

3E. Describe all the symmetries of a cube which keep one particular vertex in its original position.

3.4　Groups

The symmetry groups considered in the previous section are examples of the algebraic system known as a group. Many such examples were studied at the end of the 18th century and the beginning of the 19th century. By the end of the 19th century the important common features these examples all shared were recognised and the abstract idea of a group was formulated.

> A group G is any set of elements with a binary operation such that
>
> $ab \in G$ for all $a,b \in G$ closure property
> $(ab)c = a(bc)$ for all $a, b, c \in G$ associativity
> There is an element e of G such that
> $ae = ea = a$ for all $a \in G$ identity
> For each element a of G there is an
> element a^{-1} such that
> $aa^{-1} = a^{-1}a = e,$ inverse property

The elements of groups are conventionally denoted by lower case letters with e denoting the identity element. The symbol representing the operation is often omitted. The power -1 is conventionally used to denote taking the inverse of an element. For example, the inverse of a^{-1} is a and so $(a^{-1})^{-1} = a$.

Example 1

Prove that the set $\{1, 3, 4, 5, 9\}$ forms a group under multiplication modulo 11.
[You may assume that multiplication modulo n is associative for any n]

Solution

The group properties other than associativity are clear from the combination table.

x_{11}	1	3	4	5	9
1	1	3	4	5	9
3	3	9	1	4	5
4	4	1	5	9	3
5	5	4	9	3	1
9	9	5	3	1	4

- Closure holds because only 1, 3, 4, 5 and 9 appear in the body of the table.
- 1 is the identity element.
- 3 and 4 are inverses of each other as are 5 and 9. 1 is self-inverse.

> **Which of the following sets of numbers form groups? Justify your answers.**
>
> (a)　　All integers under subtraction.
> (b)　　$\{1, 10\}$ under multiplication modulo 11.
> (c)　　All irrational numbers under multiplication.

The challenge of group theory is to prove results about abstract groups, using just the properties of closure, associativity, identity and inverses. A few initial results of this type are given in this section.

> **The cancellation laws**
> If a, b and c are elements of a group, then
> (i) $ab = ac$ implies $b = c$;
> (ii) $ba = ca$ implies $b = c$.

The cancellation laws can be proved as follows:

$$
\begin{array}{lll}
\text{(i)} & ab = ac & \\
\Rightarrow & a^{-1}(ab) = a^{-1}(ac) & \text{premultiply by } a^{-1} \\
\Rightarrow & (a^{-1}a)b = (a^{-1}a)c & \text{associativity} \\
\Rightarrow & eb = ec & \text{inverse} \\
\Rightarrow & b = c & \text{identity}
\end{array}
$$

> **Write out a similar proof for (ii)**

The cancellation laws can be used to derive an important property of combination tables of groups with a finite number of elements.

> **The latin square property**
>
> **The combination table of any finite group is such that each row and each column consists of a permutation of the group elements.**

Example 2

Prove that the latin square property holds for any group.

Solution

This property follows from closure and the cancellation laws. Because the group is closed, any row (or column) can only contain group elements. If two elements of the row were the same then you would have a situation such as:

$$
\begin{array}{c|ccccccc}
 & \cdots & b & \cdots & c & \cdots \\
\hline
\cdot & & & & & \\
\cdot & & & & & & \text{where } ab = ac. \\
a & \cdots & ab & \cdots & ac & \cdots \\
\cdot & & & & & \\
\cdot & & & & & \\
\end{array}
$$

This contradicts the cancellation law and so no element is repeated in a row. The row therefore contains each group element precisely once.

The fact that for any positive integer n there is at least one group with n elements is investigated on the next tasksheet.

 TASKSHEET 2 — *Cyclic groups*

> **The group of integers modulo n is denoted by $\mathbb{Z}_n$.**

Each $\mathbb{Z}_n$ has combination table of the form

+	0	1	2	...	...	$n-1$
0	0	1	2	...	...	$n-1$
1	1	2	3	...	...	0
2	2	3	4	...	...	1
...	...	...	...	...	...	...

and so $\mathbb{Z}_n$ is a cyclic group.

Exercise 2

1. Explain why table (a) below cannot be a group table. Demonstrate whether or not table (b) is the combination table for a cyclic group.

(a)

	a	b	c	d
a	a	b	c	d
b	b	a	c	d
c	c	d	a	b
d	d	c	b	a

(b)

	a	b	c	d
a	b	d	a	c
b	d	c	b	a
c	a	b	c	d
d	c	a	d	b

2. Explain whether or not the following form groups:

   (a) the even integers under addition;

   (b) the odd integers under addition;

   (c) the positive real numbers under multiplication.

3. Prove that $\{1, 2, 3, 4, 5, 6\}$ is a group under multiplication modulo 7. [You may assume associativity.]

4. For the symmetry group of an equilateral triangle with reflections L, M, N and rotation R, find L^{-1}, M^{-1}, N^{-1} and R^{-1}.

5. In a group with an even number of elements, explain why there is at least one element other than the identity which is its own inverse.

3.5   Subgroups

The rotations of 0°, 120° and 240° form a group contained inside the group of symmetries of an equilateral triangle.

> **A group contained inside another group is called a subgroup.**

On the next tasksheet you will study a particular family of groups which is especially important because **every** group is a subgroup of one of these groups.

   TASKSHEET 3 – *Cayley's theorem*

On the tasksheet you met the family of permutation groups S_n. You also saw how to generate subgroups of a given group. In particular, you obtained some evidence for the following general result.

> **Any element a of a finite group with identity e generates a cyclic subgroup $\{ a, a^2, a^3, \ldots \}$. The number of elements in this subgroup is the smallest power of a which equals the identity. This number is called the order of a.**

The proof of this general result is not difficult and is given in the solutions to examples 3 and 4.

Example 3

If a is any element of a finite group G then show that there is a positive power n of a such that a^n is the identity e.

Solution

G is finite and so the infinite list $a, a^2, a^3, a^4, \ldots$ must contain repetitions. Suppose $a^l = a^k$ where $l > k$, then

$$\overbrace{a \ldots \overbrace{\qquad}^{l \text{ terms}} \ldots a}^{} = a^k$$

$$\overbrace{a \ldots a}^{l\text{-}k \text{ terms}} \; \overbrace{a \ldots a}^{k \text{ terms}} = a^k$$

$$\Rightarrow \quad a^{l-k} . a^k = e . a^k$$

$$\Rightarrow \quad a^{l-k} = e \;\; \text{(cancellation law)}$$

Example 4

If a is an element of the finite group G and if n is the order of a, then show that a generates a cyclic subgroup with n elements.

Solution

The list $e, a, a^2, \ldots, a^{n-1}$ contains n distinct elements because otherwise the method used in Example 3 would produce a power of a equal to the identity, that power being smaller than n.

The multiplication table is as shown:

	e	a	a^2	$\ldots$	a^{n-1}
e	e	a	a^2	$\ldots$	a^{n-1}
a	a	a^2	a^3	$\ldots$	e
a^2	a^2	a^3	a^4	$\ldots$	a
$\ldots$	$\ldots$	$\ldots$	$\ldots$	$\ldots$	$\ldots$

and the subgroup is therefore cyclic.

Exercise 3

1. (a) For each element of the group of symmetries of an equilateral triangle, find the cyclic subgroup it generates.

   (b) Is there an element which generates the whole group? Is the group of symmetries cyclic?

2. (a) For each element of the group $\{1, 2, 3, 4, 5, 6\}$ of integers under multiplication modulo 7, find the cyclic subgroup it generates.

   (b) Is the whole group cyclic? Justify your answer.

3. What is the identity element for the group $\{2, 4, 6, 8\}$ under multiplication modulo 10? Find all the subgroups of this group.

4. (a) Let $\{e, a, a^2, a^3\}$ be a cyclic group of order 4. How many of its elements generate this group?

   (b) How many generators are there for cyclic groups of order

       (i)   5   (ii) 6   (iii) 20?

5. If a is an element of any group, show that a and a^{-1} have the same order.

3.6   Lagrange's Theorem

On the tasksheet of the previous section you considered some subgroups of S_4. You may have noticed the curious fact that the numbers of elements in these subgroups were all divisors of 24, the number of elements in S_4.

The purpose of this section is to investigate the relationship between a group and a subgroup. You will see, both in this section and section 3.7, that knowing the structure of a subgroup helps to determine the structure of the group itself. Proceeding in this way from one group to a larger group in which it is contained is the main tool of group theorists.

The basic structural relationship can be easily seen in the case of the group S_3 of transformations of an equilateral triangle.

Let R be the clockwise rotation of 120°
and L, M and N reflections as shown.

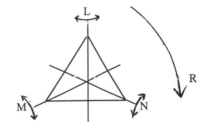

{I, R R²} is the subgroup consisting of just the rotations. The rows of the group table corresponding to elements of this subgroup are

	I	R	R²	L	M	N
I	I	R	R²	L	M	N
R	R	R²	I	M	N	L
R²	R²	I	R	N	L	M

> **List some of the things you notice about this 'cut-down' group table.**

   TASKSHEET 4 – *Group tables revisited*

In all the examples studied of a subgroup H of a finite group G, you have seen that the elements can be ordered in such a way that the rows of the group table corresponding to elements of H consist of square blocks of elements, each repeating the pattern of H. For example:

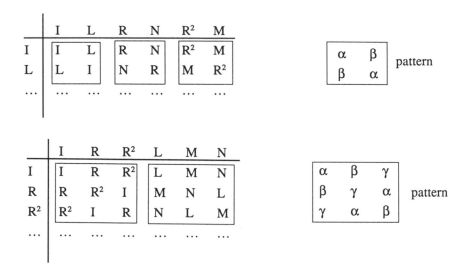

	I	L	R	N	R²	M
I	I	L	R	N	R²	M
L	L	I	N	R	M	R²
...	...	...	...	...	...	...

α	β
β	α

pattern

	I	R	R²	L	M	N
I	I	R	R²	L	M	N
R	R	R²	I	M	N	L
R²	R²	I	R	N	L	M
...	...	...	...	...	...	...

α	β	γ
β	γ	α
γ	α	β

pattern

This is **always** true and shows the remarkable way that the structure of a subgroup helps to determine the structure of the larger group. This result is extremely useful in analysing groups. One particular consequence concerns the number of elements of G (called the order of G and denoted by $|G|$).

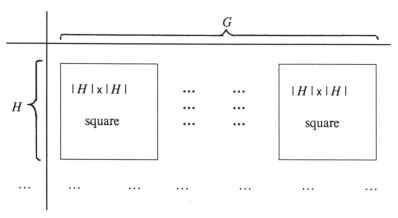

Lagrange's Theorem

If H is a subgroup of the finite group G, then $|H|$ divides $|G|$.

> **Explain how Lagrange's Theorem follows from the result about patterns of elements.**

52

Example 5

A group G has 6 elements. If a is any element of G, explain why the order of a is either 1, 2, 3 or 6.

Solution

If n is the least power of a equal to the identity, then the subgroup generated by a has n elements. Therefore, by Lagrange's Theorem, n divides 6 i.e. is 1, 2, 3 or 6.

Exercise 4

1. A group of transformations contains a reflection M and a rotation R of 90°. What is the smallest possible number of elements that the group could possess? Name such a group.

2. A combination table for 5 elements is as shown below.

	a	b	c	d	e
a	a	b	c	d	e
b	b	a	e	c	d
c	c	d	a	e	b
d	d	e	b	a	c
e	e	c	d	b	a

    (a) Show that the elements $\{a, b\}$ form a subgroup. Hence explain why the set of 5 elements cannot be a group.

    (b) Find which of the four axioms is not satisfied.

3. Use Lagrange's Theorem to help you find **all** subgroups of the group of symmetries of a square.

4. Explain why all subgroups of the group of symmetries of an equilateral triangle (other than the whole group) are cyclic.

    [Hint: let a be any non-identity element of a subgroup and consider the subgroup generated by this element.]

5. (a) If a group G has an element a of order 9, then show that G has an element of order 3.

    (b) Show that a group of order 9 must contain a cyclic subgroup of order 3.

        [Hint: consider any non-identity element a, then either a has order 3 or 9.]

    (c) Show that a group of order 27 must contain a cyclic subgroup of order 3.

3.7 Application of Lagrange's Theorem

To give you some idea of the importance of Lagrange's Theorem, two applications are considered in this section. You will see how the theorem can be used to prove a result about ordinary numbers first proved by the French mathematician Fermat in the 17th century. It will also be used to determine the nature of any group with a prime number of elements.

Fermat's result has become known as **Fermat's Little Theorem**. It can be stated as follows:

For any integer a and prime number p, $a^p - a$ is divisible by p.

> **What does Fermat's Little Theorem claim in the case when $a = 4$ and $p = 3$? Check the result in this case and one other case of your own choosing.**

A general justification for the result is outlined on the tasksheet.

   TASKSHEET 5 – *Fermat's Little Theorem*

Example 6

For any integer n, prove that $n^5 - n$ is divisible by 10.

Solution

n^5 and n are either both even or both odd and so $n^5 - n$ is divisible by 2. From Fermat's Little Theorem, $n^5 - n$ is also divisible by 5 and is therefore divisible by $2 \times 5 = 10$.

A central problem of Group Theory is to determine (as far as is possible), the nature or **structure** of all groups. Lagrange's Theorem is very useful in attempting this task as in the following example:

Example 7

Show that any group G with a prime number p of elements is cyclic.

Solution

Let e be the identity element of G and a any other element. Then the powers of a, $\{e, a, a^2, \dots\}$, form a cyclic subgroup of G with at least 2 elements. By Lagrange's Theorem the number of elements in this subgroup must divide p. Since p is prime, the subgroup has p elements and is therefore G itself.

From Example 7 you know the structure of groups with 1, 2, 3, 5 or 7 elements. Any such group must be cyclic. The structure of groups with 4 elements is studied in the following exercise.

Exercise 5

1.   The group of symmetries of a rectangle is denoted by the symbol K and is known as the Klein group after the mathematician *Klein*. Show that K is not cyclic.

2.   Let a be any element of a group G with 4 elements. Explain why the order of a is either 1, 2 or 4.

3.   Let G be any non-cyclic group of order 4 with identity e and other elements a, b and c.

     (a)   Explain why the group table has the form

	e	a	b	c
e	e	a	b	c
a	a	e		
b	b		e	
c	c			e

     (b)   Show that there is only one way of completing this group table.

Footnote

Lagrange's Theorem has given new insights into familiar concepts as with the powers of numbers considered in Fermat's Little Theorem. It has also proved to be of considerable value in group theory itself, helping to analyse the possible structures of groups.

Groups have fascinated mathematicians for nearly 200 years, as curious and interesting subjects for study in their own right. Groups have also proved to be useful as tools in some areas of science, particularly in physics and chemistry. For example, group theory has been used in investigating the molecular structure of ammonia, NH_3.

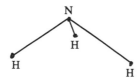

The structure is related to the symmetry group of the equilateral triangle formed by the hydrogen atoms.

Modern applications of symmetries, for example in particle physics, are beyond the scope of this unit.

3.8 Isomorphic groups

You already know that if a group has 5 elements then it is cyclic and has group table:

	I	R	R^2	R^3	R^4
I	I	R	R^2	R^3	R^4
R	R	R^2	R^3	R^4	I
R^2	R^2	R^3	R^4	I	R
R^3	R^3	R^4	I	R	R^2
R^4	R^4	I	R	R^2	R^3

$\mathbf{Z}_5$, the group of integers under addition modulo 5, has table:

	0	1	2	3	4
0	0	1	2	3	4
1	1	2	3	4	0
2	2	3	4	0	1
3	3	4	0	1	2
4	4	0	1	2	3

Clearly these two groups are **essentially** the same.

Two groups are said to be **isomorphic** if they are the same apart from the labelling of their elements. We have therefore seen that **any** group with 5 elements is isomorphic to $\mathbf{Z}_5$.

In effect, $\mathbf{Z}_5$ is the **only** group with 5 elements. In this section we will illustrate the power of Lagrange's Theorem by working out the structure of all groups with less than 8 elements.

For each number of elements any cyclic group is isomorphic to a $\mathbf{Z}_n$ and so there are the following groups:

$|G|$	1	2	3	4	5	6	7
G	$\mathbf{Z}_1$	$\mathbf{Z}_2$	$\mathbf{Z}_3$	$\mathbf{Z}_4$	$\mathbf{Z}_5$	$\mathbf{Z}_6$	$\mathbf{Z}_7$

You have also met the groups K and S_3. The purpose of this section is to determine if there any other groups with less than 8 elements.

> **Explain why there are no other groups with 1, 2, 3, 5 or 7 elements.**

Example 8

Prove that the two groups with tables as below are isomorphic.

	I	R	R^2
I	I	R	R^2
R	R	R^2	I
R^2	R^2	I	R

	a	b	c
a	c	a	b
b	a	b	c
c	b	c	a

Solution

If these are the tables of groups then they must be isomorphic because they would both be isomorphic to Z_3. This can be seen by rearranging the second table as shown:

	b	a	c
b	b	a	c
a	a	c	b
c	c	b	a

The isomorphism is now clear viz

$$I \leftrightarrow b, \quad R \leftrightarrow a, \quad R^2 \leftrightarrow c.$$

Example 9

Prove that any group G with 4 elements is isomorphic to either Z_4 or K.

Solution

If G is cyclic, then it is isomorphic to Z_4 and so you can suppose that $G = \{e, a, b, c\}$ is not cyclic.

As seen in the previous section, the group table for G is

	e	a	b	c
e	e	a	b	c
a	a	e	c	b
b	b	c	e	a
c	c	b	a	e

and all such groups must be isomorphic since this is true for **any** elements a, b and c.

The structure of groups with six elements is studied on the next tasksheet.

 TASKSHEET 6E – *Groups with 6 elements*

On Tasksheet 6E you may have seen that any group with 6 elements is either cyclic or isomorphic to S_3. The complete set of groups with less than 8 elements is:

$|G|$	1	2	3	4	5	6	7
G	$\mathbb{Z}_1$	$\mathbb{Z}_2$	$\mathbb{Z}_3$	$\mathbb{Z}_4$	$\mathbb{Z}_5$	$\mathbb{Z}_6$	$\mathbb{Z}_7$
				K		S_3	

Exercise 6

1. Classify the following groups of order 4 as isomorphic either to $\mathbb{Z}_4$ or to K, justifying your answer in each case.

    (a) The symmetries of a rectangle.

    (b) $\{2, 4, 6, 8\}$ under multiplication modulo 10.

    (c) $\{1, 3, 5, 7\}$ under multiplication modulo 8.

    (d) The numbers $\{1, -1, j, -j\}$ under multiplication, where j^2 is defined to be -1.

2. (a) How many elements does the symmetry group of a regular hexagon possess? Describe them all.

    (b) Classify all the subgroups of this group.

Note

The symmetry group of a regular hexagon has an application in studying the molecular and atomic structure of benzene. A molecule of benzene consists of a hexagonal ring of carbon atoms with hydrogen atoms attached.

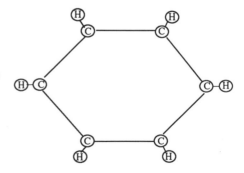

After working through this chapter you should:

1. understand how to combine symmetries of shapes and objects;

2. be able to recognise the four identifying properties of a group
    *   closure
    *   identity
    *   inverse
    *   associativity;

3. be able to generate group tables;

4. know how to identify subgroups and group elements of particular orders;

5. be able to apply Lagrange's theorem;

6. be able to recognise when two groups are isomorphic;

7. understand what is meant by a cyclic group;

8. be able to give examples of all groups of order less than 8.

Group tables

The combination table for the symmetry group of an equilateral triangle is as below where **R** is a rotation of 120° and **R²** (i.e. **R∘R**) is a rotation of 240°.

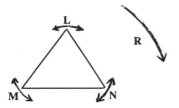

∘	I	R	R²	L	M	N
I	I	R	R²	L	M	N
R	R	R²	I	M	N	L
R²	R²	I	R	N	L	M
L	L	N	M	I	R²	R
M	M	L	N	R	I	R²
N	N	M	L	R²	R	I

1.   The above table is said to be **closed** because no new elements are produced by combinations of **I, R, R², L, M** and **N**.   Which of the tables below exhibit closure?

(i)

	a	b	c
a	c	c	c
b	b	b	b
c	a	a	a

(ii)

	a	b	c
a	a	b	c
b	b	c	a
c	c	a	b

(iii)

	a	b	c
a	I	c	b
b	c	I	a
c	b	a	I

2.   (a)   Describe how the property of being an **identity element** is evident from the table for an equilaterial triangle.

(b)   Which of the tables below include identity elements?

(i)

	a	b	c
a	c	b	a
b	a	c	b
c	b	a	c

(ii)

	a	b	c
a	a	b	c
b	c	a	b
c	b	c	a

(iii)

	a	b	c
a	c	a	b
b	a	b	c
c	b	c	a

3.   If two elements combine to form the identity element then the two elements are said to be **inverses** of each other.

(a)   List all the pairs of inverse elements for the symmetries of an equilateral triangle.

(b)   Which of the tables in question 2(b) include pairs of inverse elements?

(c)   An element can be its own inverse. For example, **L** is its own inverse because **L ∘ L = I.** What type of geometrical transformation is always its own inverse? (Such elements are called self-inverse.)

Cyclic groups

1. Draw up a combination table for the rotations I, R, R^2 of an equilateral triangle, where R is a rotation of $120°$.

2. Draw up combination tables for the rotations of regular 4-sided, 5-sided and 6-sided figures. Describe what you notice about the combination tables.

The combination table for the group of integers under addition modulo 4 is as shown

+	0	1	2	3
0	0	1	2	3
1	1	2	3	0
2	2	3	0	1
3	3	0	1	2

Successive rows follow a cyclic pattern

```
 0  1  2  3
 1  2  3  0
 2  3  0  1
etc.
```

A group whose table can be arranged to show such a pattern is called a cyclic group.

The group of integers under addition modulo n is denoted by the symbol $\mathbb{Z}_n$. You have seen that $\mathbb{Z}_4$ is a cyclic group with 4 elements. In general $\mathbb{Z}_n$ is a cyclic group with n elements.

3. Write out the group table for $\mathbb{Z}_4$ with the elements in the order 2, 1, 3, 0. Is this new table that of a cyclic group? Explain your answer.

4. (a) Describe what you think it means to say that the group of rotations of a square is **essentially the same as $\mathbb{Z}_4$**.

   (b) How many elements in the group of rotations are self-inverse? How many elements in $\mathbb{Z}_4$ are self-inverse?

5. State, with a reason, which of the following combination tables represent cyclic groups. You may need to rearrange the elements to make the table exhibit the cyclic pattern.

   (a)
	a	b	c	d
a	d	c	b	a
b	c	a	d	b
c	b	d	a	c
d	a	b	c	d

   (b)
	a	b	c	d
a	d	c	b	a
b	c	d	a	b
c	b	a	d	c
d	a	b	c	d

   (c)
	a	b	c	d
a	a	c	d	b
b	d	b	a	c
c	b	d	c	a
d	c	a	b	d

6. Determine whether $\{1, 3, 5, 7\}$ under multiplication modulo 8 forms a cyclic group.

Cayley's theorem

The first group to be considered on this tasksheet consists of all the transformations which swap the positions of three objects. To help you study this group you might like to place three numbered objects, for example playing cards, in a row.

$$\boxed{1}\quad\boxed{2}\quad\boxed{3}$$

A transformation which simply swaps the positions of objects is called a permutation. There are $3 \times 2 \times 1 = 6$ possible permutations of three objects as shown below.

You can use the following notation for particular permutations:

    s swap the positions of objects 1 and 2

    r rotate the positions of the objects so that 1 moves to 2's position, 2 moves to 3's position and 3 moves into 1's previous position.

	Permutation
$\boxed{1}\ \boxed{2}\ \boxed{3} \longrightarrow \boxed{1}\ \boxed{2}\ \boxed{3}$	e
$\boxed{1}\ \boxed{2}\ \boxed{3} \longrightarrow \boxed{1}\ \boxed{3}\ \boxed{2}$	
$\boxed{1}\ \boxed{2}\ \boxed{3} \longrightarrow \boxed{2}\ \boxed{1}\ \boxed{3}$	s
$\boxed{1}\ \boxed{2}\ \boxed{3} \longrightarrow \boxed{2}\ \boxed{3}\ \boxed{1}$	
$\boxed{1}\ \boxed{2}\ \boxed{3} \longrightarrow \boxed{3}\ \boxed{1}\ \boxed{2}$	r
$\boxed{1}\ \boxed{2}\ \boxed{3} \longrightarrow \boxed{3}\ \boxed{2}\ \boxed{1}$	

1.   Describe in words a single move equivalent to

    (a) $r^2 = r \circ r$ (b) $rs = r \circ s$ (c) $sr^2 = s \circ r \circ r$

2.   Which of the following combinations of moves are equivalent?

    (a) $r \circ r \circ s \circ r \circ s$ (b) r (c) $s \circ s \circ r \circ r \circ r \circ r$

    (d) $r \circ s \circ s \circ r \circ s$ (e) $r \circ r \circ s$ (f) $s \circ r$

3.   Find a set of rules for simplifying combinations of r and s such as $r \circ r \circ s \circ r \circ s$, $r \circ s \circ r \circ r$, etc.

4.   (a)   Explain why the set of **all** permutations of three objects forms a group with six elements.

        (b)   Show that each of the 6 elements can be obtained as combinations of r and s. [r and s are said to **generate** the group.]

        (c)   Show that r alone generates the cyclic subgroup $\{e, r, r^2\}$. Similarly, show that s alone generates the subgroup $\{e, s\}$.

(continued)

The group of permutations of n objects is denoted by S_n. You may have noticed that the group S_3 is essentially the same as the group of symmetries of an equilateral triangle. This is because the group of symmetries permutes the vertices of a triangle. Similarly, the group of symmetries of a square permutes the square's four vertices. However, not all permutations are possible e.g. no symmetry of the square swaps $\boxed{1}$ and $\boxed{2}$ whilst keeping $\boxed{3}$ and $\boxed{4}$ fixed.

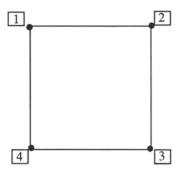

5.   (a)   Explain why S_4 has $4 \times 3 \times 2 \times 1 = 24$ elements.

(b)   The symbol $n!$ (called 'factorial' n) denotes the product $n(n-1)(n-2) \dots \times 2 \times 1$. Explain why S_n has $n!$ elements.

(c)   Show that the group of symmetries of a square contains only 8 elements of S_4.

S_4 has a large number of subgroups. For example, consider S_4 as the permutations of four objects numbered 1, 2, 3 and 4.

- The permutations which fix object 1 form a subgroup which is essentially the same as S_3.

- Other subgroups the same as S_3 are formed by permutations fixing objects 2, 3 and 4, respectively.

- S_4 contains the group of symmetries of a square.

A more reasonable task than finding all the subgroups of S_4 is to find all the subgroups of the group of symmetries of a square.

6.   Investigate the subgroups of the group of symmetries of a square. In particular, find a cyclic subgroup with four elements and find a subgroup with four elements which is not cyclic.

You have seen how some groups of symmetries can be considered to be subgroups of permutation groups. In fact, **any** group is a subgroup of an S_n for some n. This remarkable fact was first noted by the English mathematician Cayley.

Group tables revisited

The combination table for the symmetry group of an equilateral triangle is as below.

o	I	R	R²	L	M	N
I	I	R	R²	L	M	N
R	R	R²	I	M	N	L
R²	R²	I	R	N	L	M
L	L	N	M	I	R²	R
M	M	L	N	R	I	R²
N	N	M	L	R²	R	I

The rows corresponding to the elements of the subgroup $\{I, R^2, R\}$ in the order I, R², R are

o	I	R²	R	L	M	N
I	I	R²	R	L	M	N
R²	R²	R	I	N	L	M
R	R	I	R²	M	N	L

1.   Show that L, M and N can be ordered in such a way that the pattern

$$\begin{array}{ccc} \alpha & \beta & \gamma \\ \beta & \gamma & \alpha \\ \gamma & \alpha & \beta \end{array}$$

is repeated in the last 3 columns.

2.   The subgroup $\{I, L\}$ has group table

	I	L
I	I	L
L	L	I

Show that the remaining group elements can be ordered so that the first two rows of the full group table takes the form

	I	L		
I			
L			

where each 2 x 2 block has the form $\begin{array}{cc} \alpha & \beta \\ \beta & \alpha \end{array}$.

(continued)

64

3. Repeat question 2 for either the subgroup {I, M} or the subgroup {I, N}.

4. Complete the combination table below for the symmetry group of a square.

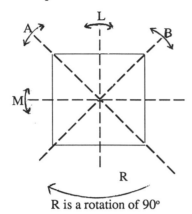

R is a rotation of 90°

	I	R	R²	R³	A	L	B	M
I	I	R	R²	R³	A	L	B	M
R	R	R²	R³	I				
R²	R²	R³	I	R				
R³	R³	I	R	R²				
A	A	M	B	L				
L	L	A	M	B				
B	B	L	A	M				
M	M	B	L	A				

5. Check that the pattern

α	β	γ	δ
β	γ	δ	α
γ	δ	α	β
δ	α	β	γ

is repeated in the top four rows of the table in question 4.

6. With respect to the subgroup {I, L, M, R²} of the group of question 4, show that the elements can be ordered so that the table is of the form

	I	L	M	R²	...	...	...	...
I	I	L	M	R²	α	β	γ	δ
L	L	I	R²	M	β	α	δ	γ
M	M	R²	I	L	γ	δ	α	β
R²	R²	M	L	I	δ	γ	β	α

7. Investigate the group table for the symmetries of a square relative to other subgroups.

Fermat's Little Theorem

1. (a) Work out the remainders when each of $0^7, 1^7, 2^7, \ldots, 6^7$ are divided by 7.

   (b) What will be the remainders when $7^7, 8^7, 9^7, \ldots$ are divided by 7?
   Explain your answer.

2. You know that $\{1, 2, 3, 4, 5, 6\}$ is a group under multiplication modulo 7. Why should you have therefore expected the result of 1(a)?

3. In what way can the result of 1 (a) be generalised to numbers other than 7?

Your work on question 1 may have convinced you that $a^7 - a$ is divisible by 7 for **any** integer a. The theorem due to Fermat, and known as Fermat's Little Theorem, states that $a^p - a$ is divisible by p for any integer a and any prime p. This can be proved formally using Lagrange's Theorem as in question 2:

4. To prove that $a^p - a$ is divisible by p for any integer a, explain why it is only necessary to consider a an element of $\{0, 1, 2, \ldots, p-1\}$.

5. $\{1, 2, \ldots, p-1\}$ forms a group with $p - 1$ elements under multiplication modulo p. Let a be any element of this group and let n be the smallest power of a which equals the identity element.

   Explain why $a^n \equiv 1$ (modulo p) and why n divides $p - 1$. Hence show that p divides $a^p - a$.

Groups with 6 elements

1. Let G be a non-cyclic group with identity element e and five other elements. Explain why any element a of G satisfies either $a^2 = e$ or $a^3 = e$.

CASE 1 - If each element a of G satisfies $a^2 = e$

2. Explain why the group table has form:

	e	a	b	c	d	f
e	e	a	b	c	d	f
a	a	e	c	b	f	d
b	b		e			
c	c			e		
d	d				e	
f	f					e

3. Explain why $(ab)(ab) = (aa)(bb)$. Hence use the cancellation law to prove that $ba = c$.

The fifth and sixth columns of the above table already contain both d and f. By the Latin square property, the second and fourth elements of the third row must therefore be d and f in some order. This contradicts $ba = c$ and shows that Case 1 cannot occur.

CASE 2 - If G has an element $a \neq e$ such that $a^3 = e$

The group table must have form:

	e	a	a^2	f	g	h
e	e	a	a^2	f	g	h
a	a	a^2	e	g	h	f
a^2	a^2	e	a	h	f	g
f	f					
g	g					
h	h					

The column for the entry for ff already contains f, g and h. f^2 is therefore e, a or a^2. Whichever of these f^2 is equal to, the column for the entry for $f.f^2$ already contains e and therefore $f^3 = f.f^2 \neq e$.

4. Explain why f^2, g^2 and h^2 are all equal to e.

5. Use $af = g$ to find gf and ga. Hence complete the table and show that it is isomorphic to that for the symmetries of an equilateral triangle.

Tutorial sheet

1. (a) For each element of the symmetry group of a rectangle, find the cyclic subgroup it generates.

    (b) Is there an element which generates the whole group? Is the group of symmetries cyclic?

2. Find a group of order 8 which has **precisely** one subgroup of order 4.

3. The simple scoreboard shown has just two squares which can each be black or white.

Three transformations are defined by

R : Flip both squares.
C_1 : Flip the left hand square.
C_2 : Flip the right hand square.

Draw up a combination table for the group generated by R, C_1 and C_2. To which well-known group is this group isomorphic?

4. Suppose that e and f are both identity elements for a particular group. Use the group properties to show that $e = f$.

5. The group of symmetries of a regular hexagon has three subgroups isomorphic to K and two subgroups isomorphic to S_3.

    (a) Each subgroup isomorphic to K can be thought of as the group of symmetries of a rectangle related to the original hexagon. Draw a hexagon showing these three rectangles.

    (b) Each subgroup isomorphic to S_3 can be thought of as the group of symmetries of an equilateral triangle related to the original hexagon. Show how these triangles are related to the hexagon.

6. A group contains an element r, of order 3, and a self-inverse element s such that $rs = sr^2$. Decide how many elements there are in the subgroup generated by r and s and draw up its group table.

4   *Mathematical proof*

4.1   Introduction

In law, proof of guilt is provided when it can be shown beyond any reasonable doubt that the charged person did indeed commit the offence.

In mathematics, proof may take many forms and some of them will be considered in this chapter. Essentially in mathematics, as in the law, the business of proof is to provide a convincing argument, based on factual evidence and sound reasoning, which shows a conjecture to be true.

In considering the following problem you will encounter a number of important mathematical ideas and gain insight into the nature of a mathematical proof.

Alice, Bob and their children Cath, Dan and Eve need to cross the river in their boat. Everyone can row but the boat will only take 1 adult or 2 children.

1.   (a)   **How can they get across?**

      (b)   **What is the least number of trips needed to get them across?**

      (c)   **How would you convince someone of your result for (b).**

2.   **Generalise your method for *m* adults and *n* children and**

      (a)   **find an algorithm for performing the transfer;**

      (b)   **show that your algorithm works;**

      (c)   **find the least possible number of trips;**

      (d)   **justify your result for (c).**

You should have been able to solve this particular problem and extend your ideas to provide a convincing argument of how the general case is solved.

'Proof is an idol before whom the mathematician tortures himself'.

A.S. Eddington

Trying to prove things which are apparently self-evident may seem strange, but there are a number of reasons why many mathematicians do just this.

•   Working on a proof can reveal new insights into a problem.

•   Working on a proof may suggest new and worthwhile areas of mathematics.

•   A convincing proof gives final authority to a conjecture and removes any doubt about whether or not it is true.

•   'Proof is … a celebration of the power of pure reason', Davis and Hersh, *The Mathematical Experience*, (Penguin Books 1981).

4.2   Direct proof

There are a number of well tried methods of directly proving things in mathematics. One method is to systematically consider every possibility. In such a proof it is essential to ensure that every possibility has been considered.

As a simple case of this, consider the statement that

> *A square number cannot have last digit 2, 3, 7 or 8.*

Suppose the square number is n^2. The whole number n ends in either 0, 1, 2, 3, 4, 5, 6, 7, 8 or 9 and so the possibilities for n are

$$n = 10k , 10k + 1, \ldots , 10k + 9.$$

If $n = 10k$, then $n^2 = 100k^2$ and so n^2 has last digit 0.

> **Explain how you know that the last digit of $100k^2$ is 0. Complete the above proof. Can you find any ways to simplify your proof?**

> **A proof where *every* possibility is considered is known as 'proof by exhaustion'.**

The following example also involves both examining every possible case **and** using algebra.

Example 1

For a prime p greater than 3, prove that $p^2 - 1$ is divisible by 12.

Solution

There are six possibilities for p modulo 6: 0, 1, 2, 3, 4 or 5. Each of these must be considered.

$p \equiv 0$, 2 or 4 (modulo 6) would imply that p is even. This is impossible.

$p \equiv 3$ (modulo 6) would imply that p is divisible by 3. A prime greater than 3 cannot be divisible by 3 and so the case $p \equiv 3$ (modulo 6) is also impossible.

If $p \equiv 1$ (modulo 6), p can be written as $6k + 1$ for some integer k. Then
$$p^2 - 1 = (6k + 1)^2 - 1 = 12 (3k^2 + k).$$
$p^2 - 1$ is therefore divisible by 12.

If $p \equiv 5$ (modulo 6), then p can be written as $6k + 5$. Then $p^2 - 1 = 12(3k^2 + 5k + 2)$.

In all possible cases, $p^2 - 1$ is divisible by 12.

Direct algebraic methods can often be used to prove **general** results.

Example 2

'A number is divisible by 3 if the sum of its digits is divisible by 3'. Prove this result for two digit numbers.

Solution

Consider the two digit number N with 10's digit a and units digit b.

$a + b$ is the sum of the two digits of the number and so you can assume that $a + b$ is divisible by 3.

Let $a + b = 3M$, where M is an integer.

$$
\begin{aligned}
\text{Then } N &= 10a + b \\
&= 9a + a + b \\
&= 9a + 3M \\
&= 3(3a + M)
\end{aligned}
$$

N therefore has a factor of 3 as required.

> **Extend the above proof to numbers with three digits.**

Exercise 1

1. (a) For n a positive integer, explain why the number $2n$ is even.

    (b) Write down, in terms of n, a number which is odd.

    (c) Prove that the sum of two odd numbers is always even.

    (d) Prove that the product of two odd numbers is always odd.

2. By considering sums of digits, find a rule for divisibility by 9 and prove it algebraically.

3. A rule for multiplying by 11 in your head is illustrated below;

$$
\begin{array}{c}
2\ 4\ 3 \times 11 \\
\swarrow\!\!\swarrow\!\!\swarrow\!\!\downarrow \\
= 2\ 6\ 7\ 3
\end{array}
$$

    (a) Investigate this rule for multiplication of two digit numbers by 11.

    (b) Prove the rule algebraically.

4. Consider the number grid shown

0	2	4	6	8	....
7	9	11	13	15	...
14	16	18	20	...	..
21	23	25	27	...	
...	...	...	..		

A typical 2 x 2 square on the grid is

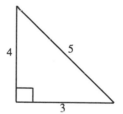

Its 'diagonal difference' is

$$11 \times 16 - 9 \times 18 = 14.$$

(a) Investigate diagonal differences for 2 x 2 squares on this grid, and conjecture a result.

(b) Prove your result algebraically.

5E A particular sequence of Pythagorean triples starts, $(3, 4, 5)$, $(5, 12, 13)$, $(7, 24, 25)$, $(9, 40, 41)$, ...

(a) Check that each triple in the sequence satisfies Pythagoras' theorem.

(b) Write down the next two triples in this sequence and check that they also satisfy Pythagoras' theorem.

(c) The first numbers of the triples form the sequence 3, 5, 7, 9, ... Write down an expression for the r th term u_r.

(d) Confirm that the r th term of the sequence 4, 12, 24, 40, ... of the second numbers of the triples is $2r(r+1)$.

(e) Write down an expression for the r th triple in this sequence of triples.

(f) Show that numbers in this sequence of triples **always** satisfy Pythagoras' theorem.

4.3   Axiomatic proof

Some of your earlier work in this unit has shown how, starting from a number of basic definitions, it is possible to build quite complicated structures. In particular you have seen some of the mathematics of groups evolve from a small number of starting properties.

A group G is any set of elements with a binary operation such that

$ab \in G$ for all $a,b \in G$ **closure property**

$(ab)c = a(bc)$ for all $a, b, c \in G$ **associativity**

There is an element e of G such that

     $ae = ea = a$ for all $a \in G$ **identity**

For each element a of G there is an

element a^{-1} such that

     $aa^{-1} = a^{-1}a = e,$ **inverse property**

Any general result about groups can be proved using just the above four properties (or **axioms**) which define a group.

Example 3

For a group G, prove that the only solution of the equation $ax = b$ is $x = a^{-1}b$.

Proof

Suppose x is a solution, then

$$ax = b$$
$$\Rightarrow \quad a^{-1}(ax) = a^{-1}b \qquad \text{(closure and inverse)}$$
$$\Rightarrow \quad (a^{-1}a)x = a^{-1}b \qquad \text{(associativity)}$$
$$\Rightarrow \qquad\quad ex = a^{-1}b \qquad \text{(inverse property)}$$
$$\Rightarrow \qquad\quad x = a^{-1}b \in G \qquad \text{(identity)}$$

> Conversely, show that $x = a^{-1}b \Rightarrow ax = b$

The results above show that $ax = b$ has unique solution $a^{-1}b$, i.e.

$$ax = b \Leftrightarrow x = a^{-1}b$$

In Chapter 3, you used the basic group axioms to prove two results known as the cancellation laws. You then used the cancellation laws to help you prove other results. This is the basic idea behind the axiomatic method of proof:

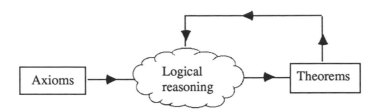

Logical reasoning from the axioms or definitions produces results known as theorems. These are, in turn, used to construct proofs of other theorems. In this way a rich mathematical field of study can blossom from a few basic definitions.

To be confident of a proof you need to be sure that your starting point is not subject to dispute and that your reasoning from that point is correct.

The first to formalise mathematics in this way were the Greeks, in particular Euclid with his treatment of geometry. The axiomatic method in geometry is illustrated in the following example. You can assume that the two results below are known and have already been proved.

(1)   angles on a straight line add to 180°

(2)   alternate angles on parallel lines are equal. i.e.

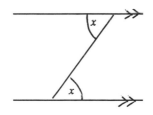

See the Bold-Shaddow of Vrania's Glory,
Immortall in his Race, no lesse in Story:
An Artist without Error, from whose Lyne,
Both Earth and Heav'ns, in sweet Proportions twine:
Behold Great EUCLID. But, behold Him well,
For 'tis in Him Divinity doth dwell.

                                        G. Wharton.

75

Example 4

To prove that the angles in a triangle add to 180°.

Proof

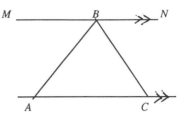

Consider triangle *ABC* shown.
Draw a line, *MN*, parallel to *AC* and through *B*.

$\angle MBA = \angle BAC$ (Result (2))

$\angle NBC = \angle BCA$ (Result (2))

$\alpha + \beta + \gamma = 180°$ (Result (1))

Therefore, the angle sum of triangle *ABC* is 180°.

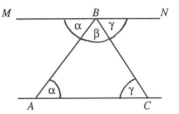

> **Use this result to show that the sum of the interior angles of a quadrilateral is 360°**

Notice that the end results are built upon previously proven results.

If you change the starting assumptions then you will inevitably end up with different results. Mathematicians do examine and change axioms, investigating the structures which result. The most famous example is in geometry where changing some of Euclid's axioms produces quite different geometries. For an interesting discussion of this you should read pages 217-223 of *'The Mathematical Experience'*, Davis and Hersh, Penguin Books, 1981.

Exercise 2

1. Prove that the exterior angle of a triangle is equal to the sum of the two opposite interior angles.

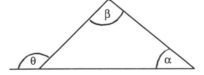

i.e. prove $\theta = \alpha + \beta$

[You can assume the results used in Example 4.]

2. (a) Prove that the angle subtended by an arc at the centre of a circle is double that subtended by the same arc at the circumference i.e. prove $\beta = 2\alpha$.

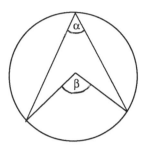

(b) List any results you need to assume in making your proof.

3. Given that a and b are two members of a group such that $ab = ba$, prove that

(a) $a^2b = ba^2$

(b) $a^{-1}b = ba^{-1}$

4. Given that a and b are any two members of a group, prove that

$$(ab)^{-1} = b^{-1}a^{-1}$$

5. An element A of a Boolean algebra is such that $A \cap X = A$ for all X. Prove that $A = \varnothing$.

6. (a) By using a Venn diagram, or otherwise, deduce a simplified form for

$$(A \cap B) \cup (A \cap B') \cup (A' \cap B) \cup (A' \cap B')$$

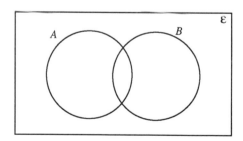

(b) Use the laws of Boolean algebra to prove your result from part (a).

4.4   Sequences of propositions

A proposition or conjecture such as

$n^2 + n + 41$ *is prime for all natural numbers n*

can be thought of as a sequence of simpler propositions

$P(1)$: $1^2 + 1 + 41$ is prime
$P(2)$: $2^2 + 2 + 41$ is prime
$P(3)$: $3^2 + 3 + 41$ is prime
... ...
... ...

To prove that the original proposition is false it is necessary only to find one value of n for which $P(n)$ is false.

Prove that the following propositions are *not* true

(a) $2^n \leq n^3 + 1$ for $n \in \mathbb{N}$

(b) $n^2 + n + 41$ is prime for $n \in \mathbb{N}$

(c) $6^n + 4n^4$ is divisible by 5 for $n \in \mathbb{N}$

(d)   When n dots on the circumference of a circle are joined by straight lines, the maximum possible number of regions is 2^{n-1}.

Many mathematical conjectures can be thought of as sequences of propositions $P(1), P(2), P(3), \ldots$ In the case of a proposition such as

$9^n + 7$ *is divisible by 8 for all natural numbers n*

it is very easy to check each individual proposition. The problem is that there are infinitely many of them!

(a)   **For the proposition**

$9^n + 7$ *is divisible by 8 for all natural numbers n*

show that P(1), P(2), P(3) and P(4) are all true.

(b)   **A computer could be programmed to check P(5), P(6), P(7), ... Explain why such a search cannot prove the original proposition.**

You can prove that a proposition is not true if you can find a single counter example. Proving a proposition to be correct, however, is not so easy. It is not good enough to assume that because you have found no evidence to the contrary that a case is proven. Mathematical proof requires more rigour.

> **Find a proposition such that P(1), P(2), ... , P(10^6) are all true but such that P(10^6 + 1) is false.**

For any particular sequence of propositions it is often very easy to decide whether each of the first few propositions are true or false. However, if they are all true, it may be far from easy to decide whether all P(n) are true or whether there is a value of k such that P(1), P(2), ..., P(k) are true but P(k + 1) is false. The problem is that k might be extremely large!

For any sequence of propositions there are three main possibilities for the truth or falsity of P(1), P(2), P(3), ...

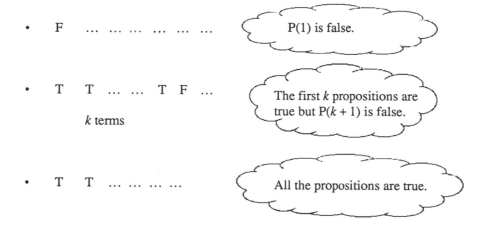

- F   ... ...   P(1) is false.

- T T ... ... T F ...   The first k propositions are true but P(k + 1) is false.

  k terms

- T T ... ...   All the propositions are true.

Many mathematical conjectures can be thought of as sequences of propositions of the form P(1), P(2), ...   Special techniques have been developed to help prove such conjectures. The method called **mathematical induction** is considered in the next section.

4.5   Mathematical induction

For any sequence of propositions, precisely one of the following must hold:

- $P(1)$ is false.
- For some k, $P(1)$, $P(2)$, ... , $P(k)$ are true but $P(k + 1)$ is false.
- All $P(n)$ are true.

> **Explain why one of the above three cases must hold for any sequence of propositions.**

Consider again the proposition

$9^n + 7$ is divisible by 8 for all natural numbers n.

You have already seen that $P(1)$ is true.

It is now necessary to check whether there is a value of k such that $P(1)$, $P(2)$, ... , $P(k)$ are true but such that $P(k + 1)$ is false.

If $P(k)$ is true then $9^k + 7$ is divisible by 8

$$\Rightarrow 9^k + 7 = 8M, \text{ where } M \text{ is an integer.}$$

Then
$$9^{k+1} + 7 = 9 \times 9^k + 7$$
$$= 9\,(8M - 7) + 7$$
$$= 72M - 56$$
$$= 8 \times (9M - 7)$$

Hence $P(k + 1)$ is also true.

The case where $P(1)$, $P(2)$, ... , $P(k)$ are all true but $P(k + 1)$ is false cannot occur and so $P(n)$ is true for all natural numbers n.

An argument such as the one above is called a proof by **mathematical induction**.

> **Mathematical induction is a method of proving that every member of a sequence of propositions is true. Such a proof takes the form:**
>
> - **$P(1)$ is shown to be true.**
> - **$P(k + 1)$ is shown to be true whenever $P(1)$, $P(2)$, ... , $P(k)$ are true.**

Mathematical induction is useful whenever you can use the truth of $P(k)$ to prove $P(k + 1)$.

Example 5

Prove that the sum of the first n odd numbers is n^2.

Solution

$1 = 1^2$, so P(1) is true.

Assume P(k) is true. The sum of the first k odd numbers is therefore k^2

   i.e. $1 + 3 + 5 + \ldots + (2k - 1) = k^2$.

Then the sum of the first k +1 odd numbers is

$$1 + 3 + 5 + \ldots + (2k - 1) + 2k + 1$$

$$= \qquad k^2 \qquad\qquad + 2k + 1$$
$$= \qquad (k + 1)^2$$

Hence P(k + 1) is true. By induction, the sum of the first n odd numbers is n^2 for all natural numbers n.

Formulae for sums of series can often be proved using mathematical induction because the sum of $k + 1$ terms of a series is simply the sum of k terms plus the $k + 1$th term. The following example demonstrates mathematical induction in another context.

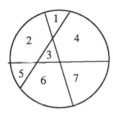

A circular pie is divided by repeatedly making straight cuts. Find a fomula for the maximum number of pieces after n cuts. For example, 3 cuts produce at most 7 pieces.

A table for the number of helpings produced by n cuts is as shown.

number of cuts, n	:	1	2	3	4	...
number of helpings, h_n	:	2	4	7	11	...

This sequence of numbers for h_n is similar to the sequence of triangle numbers

   1, 3, 6, 10 ...

and so it is reasonable to conjecture that $h_n = 1 + \frac{1}{2} n (n + 1)$.

To prove such a conjecture by induction it is necessary to find an inductive linkage between h_k and h_{k+1}.

After k cuts have been made, the $k+1$th cut produces as many additional pieces as possible only if it cuts each of the previous cuts.

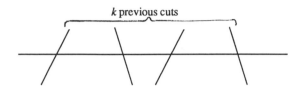

k previous cuts

> **Explain why it therefore follows that $h_{k+1} = h_k + k + 1$.**

Once this linkage has been established it is straightforward to prove the conjecture.

Example 6

The greatest possible number of helpings after n cuts is $h_n = 1 + \frac{1}{2} n (n + 1)$.

Solution

After 1 cut there are two pieces. So $h_1 = 2 = 1 + \frac{1}{2} \times 1 \times 2$. P(1) is therefore true.

Assume P(k) is true, i.e. $h_k = 1 + \frac{1}{2} k (k + 1)$.

Then $h_{k+1} = h_k + k + 1$
$$= 1 + \frac{1}{2} k (k + 1) + k + 1$$
$$= 1 + (k + 1)(\frac{1}{2} k + 1)$$
$$= 1 + \frac{1}{2} (k + 1)(k + 2)$$

Hence P(k + 1) is true.

By mathematical induction, $h_n = 1 + \frac{1}{2} n (n + 1)$ for all natural numbers n.

Exercise 3

1. Prove by mathematical induction that numbers of the form $8^n + 6$ are divisible by 14 for all natural numbers n .

2. A special case of Fermat's Little Theorem (see Chapter 3) is that $n^3 - n$ is divisible by 3 for all natural numbers n. Prove this result by mathematical induction.

3. Use mathematical induction to show that $1 + 2 + 3 + ... + n = \frac{n}{2} (n + 1)$.

4. Prove that $1^3 + 2^3 + 3^3 + ... + n^3 = \frac{n^2}{4} (n + 1)^2$.

5. Prove that $\frac{1}{1 \times 2} + \frac{1}{2 \times 3} + ... + \frac{1}{n(n+1)} = \frac{n}{n+1}$

6. Prove that the sum of the cubes of 3 consecutive integers is always divisible by 9.

4.6   Proof by contradiction

In many situations it can be easier to consider the alternative(s) to that which you are trying to prove and show that it leads to a contradiction. This is an important method of proof and is illustrated in the following example.

'By a process of elimination ...'

Example 7

Show that, if a^2 is even, then a is even.

Solution

Consider the alternative, that there is an odd number a such that a^2 is even.

Let $a = 2n + 1$

> **Explain why any odd number can be expressed in the form $2n + 1$.**

Then
$$a^2 = (2n + 1)^2$$
$$= 4n^2 + 4n + 1$$
$$= 4n(n + 1) + 1$$

The number on the right of this expression is an **odd** number and so a^2 is odd.

> **Explain how you know that $4n(n+ 1) + 1$ is odd.**

However, this is a **contradiction.**   The alternative is therefore impossible and you can conclude that if a^2 is even, then a is even.

In the Greek world, the claim made by Pythagoras that $\sqrt{2}$ was irrational caused an enormous philosophical upheaval in the intellectual community. The following proof of this claim uses the result proved in Example 7.

Assume $\sqrt{2}$ is rational.

Then $\sqrt{2} = \dfrac{a}{b}$ (where a, b have **no** common factors).

$\Rightarrow 2 = \dfrac{a^2}{b^2}$

$\Rightarrow 2b^2 = a^2$

So a^2 is even and therefore a is even.

Let $a = 2m$ $(m \in \mathbb{N})$

Then $a^2 = 4m^2$

$\Rightarrow 2b^2 = 4m^2$

$\Rightarrow b^2 = 2m^2$

$\Rightarrow b$ is even

Since a and b are both even, they have a common factor of 2. This **contradicts** the initial statement that a and b have **no** common factors. Hence $\sqrt{2}$ cannot be rational.

A good way of checking your understanding of a proof is to prove for yourself another very similar result.

> **Show that $\sqrt{5}$ is irrational. What happens when you attempt to prove $\sqrt{9}$ is irrational?**

 TASKSHEET 1 - *Some proofs using contradiction*

Prime numbers have fascinated mathematicians for centuries. Their study is important, both in mathematics and in real world applications. For example, the unit *Information and coding* provides illustrations of the applications of prime numbers in secret codes. An excellent discussion of the role of prime numbers in secret codes and modern day computer applications may be found in *Mathematics : The New Golden Age*, Keith Devlin, (Penguin Books).

The method of proof by contradiction is a very important one in mathematics and is the basis for the proof of many great results.

4.7　Mathematics and computers

To produce sensible conjectures and to decide how to set about proving them, Mathematicians need information. For example, you have already seen that there are infinitely many primes, but before making further conjectures about the distribution of primes it would be sensible to have more data than just a knowledge of a handful of small primes such as 2, 3, 5, 7 and 11.

The notation conventionally used to denote the number of primes less than a number N is $\pi(N)$. A computer can easily be programmed to generate a table of values of $\pi(N)$ such as the following:

N	$\pi(N)$
10	4
10^2	25
10^3	168
10^4	1229
10^5	9592
10^6	78 498
10^7	664 579
10^8	5 761 455
10^9	50 847 534
10^{10}	455 052 512

There are 25 primes less than 100.

In 1792, the 15 year old Gauss used Lambert's table of primes up to 10^5 to correctly conjecture the result now known as the Prime Number Theorem,

$$\pi(N) \approx \frac{N}{\ln N} \ .$$

> (a)　Show that $\pi(10) = 4$.
>
> (b)　Find the 168th prime number.
>
> (c)　Use a calculator or short program and the above table of values of $\pi(N)$ to check the Prime Number Theorem.

Information from a table such as the one above does not **prove** the Prime Number Theorem and it was over 100 years after Gauss first conjectured the result before it was eventually proved.

As well as helping you to formulate conjectures, computers can be useful even in **proving** results. For example, they can be especially valuable when, as in some of the problems of section 4.2, you need to check a number of cases. So far, their most renowned use in this respect has been in the proof of the Four Colour Conjecture.

When colouring a map of countries, it is natural to ensure that countries with a common border are coloured differently. Many people who have tried this will have noted that at most four colours are needed, no matter how complicated the map. As a mathematical problem requiring proof, the idea that four colours can be used to colour any map drawn on a plane surface was first conjectured by Augustus de Morgan in 1852.

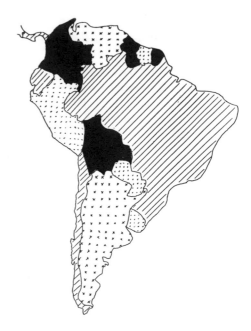

> **(a)** **Find a four colouring of the South American map shown above, treating the sea as a 'country'.**
>
> **(b)** **Find a map drawn on a torus (a ring doughnut) which requires 5 colours.**

In 1879, Alfred Kempe published a proof of the Four Colour Conjecture. Kempe assumed that there was a map which could **not** be four coloured and then considered such a map with the smallest possible number of countries. Kempe could therefore assume that all maps with fewer regions **could** be four coloured. This fact was then used to deduce results about the supposed counterexample.

> **What type of proof did Kempe use?**

Kempe's proof unfortunately contained an error which was pointed out by Percy Heawood in 1890. From then on, many mathematicians attempted a proof and more and more results were obtained about a minimal counterexample.

In 1976, Kenneth Appel and Wolfgang Haken finally showed that a minimal counterexample could not exist. Their procedures involved consideration of so many different cases that they relied heavily on computer testing of possibilities for the supposed counterexample. A good description of their work and of Kempe's 'proof' is given in *Mathematics Review, Volume 1, Nos 1 and 2, Philip Allan Publishers*.

Although the Four Colour Conjecture has now been proved, there are still many famous unproven conjectures, as you will discover on the next tasksheet.

TASKSHEET 2 - *Some famous conjectures*

On the tasksheet you met an example of how computers are used in number theory to look for counterexamples. It should also be mentioned that computers are starting to be used in the area of axiomatic proof which you considered in section 4.3. They can be programmed to both generate and check chains of logical reasoning from geometrical or other axioms. In the long term, it is this development which may have the most fundamental effect upon rigour within mathematical argument.

After working through this chapter you should:

1.   appreciate the need for rigorous proofs;

2.   be able to make direct proofs by, for example,

   •   considering every possible case;
   •   using algebra;

3.   be able to formulate simple axiomatic proofs;

4.   be able to use the method of mathematical induction;

5.   be able to conduct a proof by contradiction;

6.   appreciate that computers can be used to

   •   obtain information which can stimulate new discoveries;
   •   make a case-by-case analysis of a situation;
   •   seek counterexamples;
   •   generate and check axiomatic proofs.

Some proofs using contradiction

A first question when considering prime numbers is to wonder just how many of them there are. A very ancient proof, accredited to the Greek mathematician Euclid, is a good illustration of the method of proof by contradiction.

Problem - to prove that there are an infinite number of prime numbers.

It is very difficult to get hold of anything to work with from this statement and so you can consider the alternative statement to see if this helps.

Solution

Suppose there is a **finite** number of primes, and the complete list of all primes is

$$2, 3, 5, 7, 11, 13, \ldots , p_n .$$

Consider the product of all these primes plus one.

i.e. $N = (2 \times 3 \times 5 \times 7 \times \ldots \times p_n) + 1$

N is either prime or divisible by a prime.

It is clear that N has remainder 1 when divided by 2 and therefore 2 cannot be a factor of N. By the same token, N is not divisible by 3 or 5 or 7 ... or any prime number in the list of primes.

This contradicts the assumption that the list of primes is complete and so the list of primes can **never** be complete and so must be an infinite list.

The largest **known** prime number (in 1991) is $2^{216091} - 1$.

Euclid's proof is an instructive example of proof by contradiction. There are two clear alternatives:

- there is an infinite number of primes;

or

- there is a finite number of primes.

The first alternative is what you want to prove but it cannot be proved directly. The second alternative gives you something definite to work with - a list of all the primes, $2, 3, \ldots, p_n$.

Proof by contradiction is exactly like a detective's process of elimination. The alternative(s) are thoroughly investigated. If they can be shown to be impossible then you have the proof you require.

(continued)

Prime numbers are especially important because **every** integer greater than 1 is either prime or can be expressed as a product of prime factors.

For example, $24 = 2 \times 12$
$= 2 \times 2 \times 6$
$= 2 \times 2 \times 2 \times 3$
So $24 = 2^3 \times 3$

Further, you may know that however you go about factorising the number, you always end up with the same prime factors. This is known as the Unique Factorisation Theorem.

1.   Factorise 138 in two different ways and confirm that in each case you end up with the same prime factors.

You are now in a position to consider an alternative proof, again by contradiction, that $\sqrt{2}$ is irrational.

Assume the alternative, that $\sqrt{2} = \dfrac{a}{b}$

Then $2b^2 = a^2$

If the prime factors of a are $f_1 f_2 f_3 \dots f_n$ say, then

a^2 has prime factors $(f_1 f_1)(f_2 f_2) \dots$ etc.

Similarly b^2 has prime factors $(p_1 p_1)(p_2 p_2) \dots$

Then $2b^2$ has an odd number of prime factors whereas a^2 has an even number of prime factors.

2.   Explain why this is a contradiction and therefore why $\sqrt{2}$ cannot be a rational number.

3.   Use this method to show that $\sqrt{5}$ is irrational

Some famous conjectures

Occasionally mathematics makes headlines in the national press. The following is part of an article from *The Guardian* on a possible proof of perhaps the most famous of all unproven conjectures, Fermat's Last Theorem.

Mathematician's answer to old puzzle fails to add up

By Tom Wilkie
Science Correspondent

The most celebrated unsolved puzzle in mathematics, Fermat's Last Theorem, seems to have defeated the latest attempt at a solution.

Dr. Yoichi Miyaoka, a Japanese mathematician working at the Max Planck Institute for Mathematics in Bonn, West Germany, put forward a draft solution in the course of a three-hour lecture on 26 February. But Dr. Miyaoka was very cautious and tentative, refusing to claim that he had cracked the problem until his methods had been checked and verified by other mathematicians.

It now appears that his caution was justified. Close inspection of the proof appears to have thrown up obstacles and Dr. Miyaoka has tentatively withdrawn the proof.

For more than 350 years, professional mathematicians, amateurs and outright cranks have tried to solve Fermat's theorem. It seems like a maddeningly simple extension of the classroom classic, Pythagoras' theorem, but it has defeated all attempts at solution.

The story is now famous: in 1637, the French lawyer and amateur mathematician Pierre de Fermat jotted the theorem down in the margin of the book he was reading, with the note, "I have discovered a truly remarkable proof which this margin is too small to contain".

The list of mathematicians who have tried their hand at solving the theorem reads like a roll call of the greatest and best. Even the German mathematician Carl Friedrich Gauss, who somewhat petulantly declared that the theorem did not interest him, had a go at proving part of it.

Cranks have been spurred on by the prospects of two substantial prizes that have been offered for solving the theorem. In 1850, the *Academie des Sciences* in Paris offered a gold medal and FR3,000 as a reward. In 1908, the German Dr. Paul Wolfskehl bequeathed 100,000 marks as a prize, to be administered by the University of Gottingen. Inflation in Weimar Germany eroded the value of the prize, which now stands at DM10,000 (about £3,000).

The theorem concerns integers - whole numbers like 1, 2, 3, etc - and the sum of their squares (or cubes, or quadrates, and so on).

Pierre de Fermat: His 'remarkable proof' of 1637 has defeated all attempts to solve it.

The sum of two squared integers can itself be an integer squared:
$$3^2 + 4^2 = 5^2$$
But can the sum of two cubes itself be a cube? Can the sum of two integers raised to the fourth power be an integer raised to the fourth power?

Fermat claimed that only in the Pythagorean case ($n = 2$) could the equation:
$$x^n + y^n = z^n$$
have solutions where x, y, z were integers. For all values of n greater than 2, Fermat asserted, the equation had no non-zero integer solutions.

In 1983, the hunt for a proof took a great leap forward. The German mathematician Gerd Faltings solved a different problem - Mordell's conjecture. A consequence of this proof was that, if Fermat is wrong, then there are at most a finite number of counterexamples for each value of n. (Fermat of course said that the number of counterexamples was finite and precisely equal to zero).

But, according to Dr. Charles Matthews, a mathematician at Cambridge University, Faltings "did not show how to get hold of any of the solutions, if they did exist".

Guardian November 1989

(continued)

The following are some other conjectures, none of which has yet been proven. You might like to investigate one or two of them.

- Every even number bigger than 4 may be expressed as the sum of two prime numbers. (This is the famous Goldbach conjecture.)

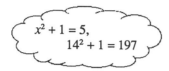

$$74 = 13 + 61$$
$$12 = 5 + 7$$

- There are infinitely many prime numbers of the form $n^2 + 1$ for $n \in Z^+$.

$$x^2 + 1 = 5,$$
$$14^2 + 1 = 197$$

- There are infinitely many twin primes. (Twin primes are primes that differ by 2.)

$$\{11, 13,\} \qquad \{107, 109\}$$
$$\{17, 19\}$$

- There is always a prime number between consecutive squares n^2 and $(n + 1)^2$.

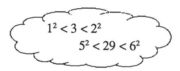

$$1^2 < 3 < 2^2$$
$$5^2 < 29 < 6^2$$

If counterexamples exist to any of the above conjectures then they would have to be very large indeed. Using computers to search for counterexamples is not just a crude process of blind searching because of the time this would take. Trying to obtain a counterexample to the following conjecture will show you how difficult such searches can be.

In the eighteenth century, Euler conjectured a generalisation of Fermat's Last Theorem.

For $n \geq 3$, the equation $x_1^n + x_2^n + \ldots + x_{n-1}^n = x_n^n$ has no solution in positive integers.

The first counterexample to Euler's conjecture was found, using a computer, in 1966. See if you can find this counterexample - you have the advantage of being given $n = 5$ and knowing that each of a, b, c and d is less than 144.

Problem

Find four positive integers, a, b, c and d such that $a^5 + b^5 + c^5 + d^5 = 144^5$.
(A counterexample to Euler's conjecture with $n = 5$.)

Tutorial sheet

Attempt to prove or disprove each of the following conjectures.

1. Any whole number greater than 7 can be expressed in the form $3m + 5n$, for non-negative integers m and n.

2. There is no smallest positive number.

3. The numbers 7, 37, 337, 3337, ... are all prime.

4. The numbers 49, 4489, 444889, 44448889, ... are all perfect squares.

5. The interior angles of an n-sided polygon sum to $2n - 4$ right angles.

6. $1 \times n + 2(n - 1) + 3(n - 2) + \ldots + n \times 1 = \frac{1}{6}n(n + 1)(n + 2)$.

7. Two players take it in turn to remove 1, 2 or 3 matches from a large pile of matches. The player who takes the last match is the winner.

One of the players claims that she can always win when left a pile containing an odd number of matches. Is she right?

SOLUTIONS

1 Binary operations

1.1   Structure

> **Explain the above statement for the game of 'noughts and crosses'.**

The first O can be placed either in a corner or in the middle of an edge. By symmetry (a structural idea) it does not matter **which** corner or **which** edge.

A corner move

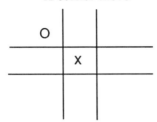

An edge move

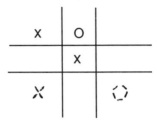

There are now four possible different X moves but O can always draw.

O must play at ⟨⟩
Then X wins.

1.2   Notation for transformations

> **What notation helps to explain the impossibility?**

If 1 represents an upright tumbler and 0 one which is upside down, then the sum starts as 0.

Every turn changes the sum by 0 or 2 so you can never obtain the odd sum 3, which is required.

> If L ∘ R means *perform* R *and then* L, describe the transformation L ∘ R. Similarly, describe L ∘ L, R ∘ R and R ∘ L.
>
> Denoting L ∘ R by O and L ∘ L by N, copy and complete the table below.

L ∘ R and **R ∘ L** have the same effect as turning over the outside pair of tumblers. **L ∘ L** and **R ∘ R** have the same effect as doing nothing.

	L	R
L	N	O
R	O	N

Complete the table.

What extra elements have now been obtained?

How does this show that the three tumblers _cannot_ all be turned right way up?

	N	L	R	O
N	N	L	R	O
L	L	N	O	R
R	R	O	N	L
O	O	R	L	N

No extra elements have been obtained. So any combination of turns from the original position is equivalent to either **N, L, R,** or **O**. None of these results in the tumblers all being upright.

Find l ∘ l, m ∘ m, r ∘ r and l ∘ m.

l ∘ l = I

m ∘ m = I

r ∘ r = I

l ∘ m = r

The result of performing any transformation of the rectangle twice is the identity transformation and similarly for any turn of the tumblers.

Write down at least one other result which must hold for both the rectangle and the tumblers.

There are a number of results which you may have noticed, two of which are noted below.

• The result of performing any two consecutive transformations is not affected by the order of these transformations

      e.g.   l ∘ m = m ∘ l .

• The result of performing two consecutive, non-identity, non-equal transformations is always the third non-identity transformation.

      e.g.   l ∘ m = r

             r ∘ l = m   etc.

1.3 Isomorphic structures

> **To convince yourself that this does establish the equivalence of the two games, what must you check now?**

You must check that any 'line' corresponds to three numbers with a sum of 15 and, conversely, that any set of three numbers with a sum of 15 corresponds to a 'line'.

> **How can you tell from the combination table that all combinations correspond appropriately?**

In one of the combination tables you can replace all letters by their corresponding letters.

E.g.

	I	l	m	r
I	I	l	m	r
l	l	I	r	m
m	m	r	I	l
r	r	m	l	I

→

	N	L	R	O
N	N			
L		N		
R			N	
O				N

etc.

This must result in the other combination table (or a simple rearrangement of it as in Example 2).

> **Show that $0 \leftrightarrow b$, $1 \leftrightarrow c$, $2 \leftrightarrow a$ also sets up an isomorphism between (a) and (b).**

	0	1	2
0	0	1	2
1	1	2	0
2	2	0	1

→

	b	c	a
b	b	c	a
c	c	a	b
a	a	b	c

These rows and columns can be reordered to give:

	a	b	c
a	c	a	b
b	a	b	c
c	b	c	a

as required.

Exercise 1

1.

∘	I	A	B	C	D	E
I	I	A	B	C	D	E
A	A	B	I	D	E	C
B	B	I	A	E	C	D
C	C	E	D	I	B	A
D	D	C	E	A	I	B
E	E	D	C	B	A	I

2.

∘	I	R	S	L	M	N
I	I	R	S	L	M	N
R	R	S	I	M	N	L
S	S	I	R	N	L	M
L	L	N	M	I	S	R
M	M	L	N	R	I	S
N	N	M	L	S	R	I

3.   The tables are identical apart from the symbols being used. From table 1 to table 2, letters have been changed as $I \rightarrow I$, $A \rightarrow R$, $B \rightarrow S$, $C \rightarrow L$, $D \rightarrow M$, and $E \rightarrow N$.

Dienes' game and the rotations and reflections of an equilateral triangle have **isomorphic** structures.

4.   Some of the many features you may have noticed are:

• each element occurs precisely once in every row;

• each element occurs precisely once in every column;

• the table is symmetrical about the main diagonal ⤢ ;

• each element on the main diagonal is **I**;

• an $\begin{array}{cc} x & y \\ y & x \end{array}$ pattern is repeated four times, viz. ▢▢ ▢▢

5. Some of the many features you may have noticed are:

- each element occurs precisely once in every row;

- each element occurs precisely once in every column;

- the table is **not** symmetrical about the main diagonal;

- an $\begin{array}{ccc} x & y & z \\ y & z & x \\ z & x & y \end{array}$ pattern is repeated twice on the top 3 rows;

- an $\begin{array}{ccc} x & y & z \\ z & x & y \\ y & z & x \end{array}$ pattern is repeated twice on the bottom 3 rows.

1.4 Elements and operations

> (a) **Why is it impossible to write down the whole combination table?**
>
> (b) **State some of the features of each of the two tables above.**

(a) Because there are infinitely many elements.

(b) Some of the many features you may have noticed are:

- The addition table only contains the original elements (the whole numbers) whereas the division table generates new elements (fractions).

- The rows of the addition table are formed from each other by shifts:

$$\ldots \quad a \quad b \quad c \quad \ldots$$

$$\ldots \quad a \quad b \quad c \quad \ldots$$

- The addition table is symmetrical about the main diagonal but the division table is not

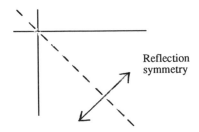

Reflection symmetry

98

Exercise 2

1.   (a) +   (b) –   (c) x   (d) ↑

2.   (a) 8   (b) $9\frac{1}{2}$ (c) $2\frac{1}{2}$ (d) 10

3.   (a) $3x^2 - 4x + 6$ (b) $x^3 + 3x^2 - 6x + 6$

    (c) $2x^4 - x^3 - 8x^2 + 6x - 1$ (d) $2x^4 - x^3 - 8x^2 + 6x - 1$

4.   fg: $x \rightarrow 2(x - 1) = 2x - 2$

    gf: $x \rightarrow 2x - 1$

The elements are the functions f and g.

The operation is the conventional 'function of a function' rule for combining functions.

5.

	I	P	Q
I	I	P	Q
P	P	Q	I
Q	Q	I	P

1.5   Clock or modulo arithmetic

> **Think of conventional clocks and describe why it is sensible to write symbolised statements such as**
>
> (a) $10 + 4 = 2$ (b) $1 - 5 = 8.$

(a)   4 hours after 10 o'clock it is 2 o'clock.

(b)   5 hours before 1 o'clock it is 8 o'clock.

Complete the combination table for this clock.

+	0	1	2	3
0				
1				
2			0	1
3				

+	0	1	2	3
0	0	1	2	3
1	1	2	3	0
2	2	3	0	1
3	3	0	1	2

Explain some of the entries in the above combination table.

A typical explanation might be:

4 x 3 = 12 which is the same as 2 when you subtract 5's.

Exercise 3

1.

+	0	1	2	3	4	5
0	0	1	2	3	4	5
1	1	2	3	4	5	0
2	2	3	4	5	0	1
3	3	4	5	0	1	2
4	4	5	0	1	2	3
5	5	0	1	2	3	4

2.

+	0	1
0	0	1
1	1	0

3.

+	E	O
E	E	O
O	O	E

This table is isomorphic to that of question 2:

$0 \rightarrow E$
$1 \rightarrow O$

100

4.

+	0	1	2	3
0	0	1	2	3
1	1	2	3	0
2	2	3	0	1
3	3	0	1	2

x	1	2	4	3
1	1	2	4	3
2	2	4	3	1
4	4	3	1	2
3	3	1	2	4

The isomorphism is $0 \to 1$; $1 \to 2$; $2 \to 4$; $3 \to 3$;
(Also possible is $0 \to 1$; $1 \to 3$; $2 \to 4$; $3 \to 2$)

5. Several possible reasons could be given. One simple reason is that each transformation of a rectangle combines with itself to form the identity element but this is not true for addition modulo 4. e.g. $1 + 1 \neq 0$ (modulo 4).

1.6 Does the order matter?

> **For all possible pairs of moves in the tumblers problem show that the order of the moves does not matter.**
>
> **Why can you be certain that this is also true of the transformations of a rectangle?**

The table for the tumblers problem is

∘	N	R	L	O
N	N	R	L	O
R	R	N	O	L
L	L	O	N	R
O	O	L	R	N

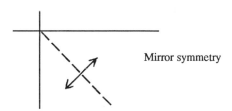

Mirror symmetry

For any pair of elements a and b it is apparent that $a \circ b = b \circ a$ because the table is symmetrical about the main diagonal.

Because of the isomorphism established earlier, any result which is true for the tumblers must also be true for the transformations.

All pairs of elements for which *a* or *b* is *I*.

All pairs of elements for which *a* = *b*.

Also $R \circ S = S \circ R$

For example $(12 - 6) - 3 = 3$,

whereas $12 - (6 - 3) = 9$.

Also $(12 \div 6) \div 3 = \frac{2}{3}$,

whereas, $12 \div (6 \div 3) = 6$

Exercise 4

1.   (a)   2   (b)   4   (c)   125   (d)   0

     (e) $3\theta\, 1 = 9$ (f) $1\theta\, 9 = 9$ (g)   8   (h)   –8

     (i) $2\theta\, 3 = 12$ (j) $^-1\theta\, 12 = 12$

     $1\, \theta\, 2 \neq 2\, \theta\, 1$ and so $a\, \theta\, b = b\, \theta\, a$ does not hold for **all** *a* and *b*.

     $(2\, \theta\, 1)\, \theta\, 1 \neq 2\, \theta\, (1\, \theta\, 1)$ and so $a\, \theta\, (b\, \theta\, c) = (a\, \theta\, b)\, \theta\, c$ does not hold for **all** *a*, *b* and *c*.

2.   (a)   No.   E.g. $1 * 2 \neq 2 * 1$

     (b)   No.   E.g. $1 * (0 * 0) \neq (1 * 0) * 0$

3.   *G* is commutative because the greater of two numbers is independent of the order in which they are written down.

     Similarly, the greatest of three numbers is independent of which pair is compared first, and so *G* is associative.

4.   (a)   All possible pairs of *a* and *b*.

     (b)   Just one counter example is sufficient to establish non-commutativity.

5E.   Establishing that $(a * b) * c$ for one particular choice of *a*, *b* and *c* does **not** prove that * is associative. To prove associativity you must either consider **all** possible choices of *a*, *b* and *c* or find some general reason.

    The combination of **any** transformations is associative because $(a * b) * c$ and $a * (b * c)$ both mean' do *c*, then do *b*, then do *a*.'

6E.   (a)   Denote the operation of addition modulo *n* by $\oplus$. For any elements *a* and *b*, $a \oplus b$ is either equal to $a + b$ or differs from it by a multiple of *n*. Similarly, $b \oplus a$ either equals $b + a$ or differs from it by a multiple of *n*.

         Since $a + b = b + a$, $a \oplus b$ either equals $b \oplus a$ or differs from it by a multiple of *n*. However, $a \oplus b$ and $b \oplus a$ are both in the set $\{0, 1, \ldots , n - 1\}$ and so cannot differ from each other by any multiple of *n* other than zero. Hence $a \oplus b = b \oplus a$ and addition modulo *n* is commutative.

    (b)   Similarly, $(a \oplus b) \oplus c$ and $u \oplus (b \oplus c)$ are each either equal to $a + b + c$ or differ from it by a multiple of *n*.

         Since $(a \oplus b) \oplus c$ and $a \oplus (b \oplus c)$ are both in the set $\{ 0, 1, \ldots, n - 1\}$ they cannot differ from each other by any multiple of *n* other than zero.

         Hence $(a \oplus b) \oplus c = a \oplus (b \oplus c)$ for any elements *a*, *b* and *c*. $\oplus$ is therefore associative.

2 Set algebra

2.1 Set notation

In the class there are twenty-five children. Eight children play the piano and of these five also play the violin. Eleven children play neither piano nor violin. Use the diagram to determine how many children play the violin.

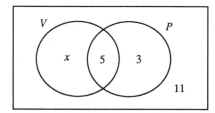

5 children play the violin **and** the piano. These are marked in the 'overlap' region on the diagram. As there are 8 children who play the piano, there must be 3 children who play the piano but not the violin. These are also marked on the diagram and so are the 11 children who play neither instrument.

If x children play the violin but not the piano, then

$$x + 5 + 3 + 11 = 25 \qquad \text{(as there are 25 children in the class).}$$

Then $x = 6$ and $6 + 5 = 11$ children play the violin.

Explain why

(a) $\quad 0 \leq n\,(F) \leq 11$ (b) $\quad 0 \leq n\,(C) \leq 6$

(a) The Venn diagram shows that children who play the flute do not play the piano or the violin. There are 11 children in this category, but there is no information as to how many of them play the flute. The number of children who play the flute can, therefore, be anything from 0 to 11.

(b) The Venn diagram shows that children who play the cello all play the violin but not the piano. There are 6 children in this category and so $0 \leq n\,(C) \leq 6$.

(a) $\{\,11,\ 13,\ 17,\ 19\,\}$

(b) $\{\,1,\ 2,\ 3,\ 4,\ 5,\ 6,\ 7,\ 8\,\}$

(a) $P \cup P' = \varepsilon$ so $n\,(P \cup P') = n\,(\varepsilon)$

(b) Pupils who play the piano but not the violin.

(c)

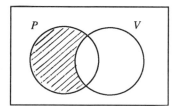

Exercise 1

1. (a) $S \cap S' = \varnothing$ (b) $S \cup S' = \varepsilon$

     (c) $(S')' = S$ (d) $\varnothing' = \varepsilon$

2. (a)

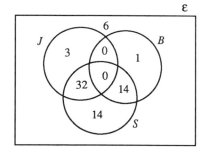

ε represents the set of children who wear a white shirt

S represents the set of children who wear a skirt

S' represents the set of children who wear trousers

B represents the set of children who wear a blazer

J represents the set of children who wear a jumper.

(b) $n\,(\varepsilon) = 3 + 6 + 1 + 32 + 14 + 14 = 70$

     There were 70 children on the outing.

3. Let the number who participate in all three sports be x. Then the Venn diagram can be completed in terms of x.

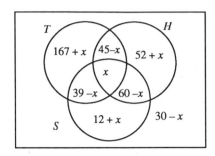

From the diagram it can be seen that x, the number of pupils who play all three sports, can be any number from 0 to 30.

4.

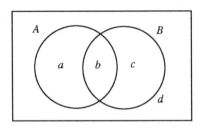

If the numbers of elements in the different parts of the Venn diagram are a, b, c and d as shown, then

$$a + b + c = (a + b) + (b + c) - b$$

$$\Rightarrow \quad n(A \cup B) = n(A) + n(B) - n(A \cap B)$$

$$\Rightarrow \quad \frac{n(A \cup B)}{n(\varepsilon)} = \frac{n(A)}{n(\varepsilon)} + \frac{n(B)}{n(\varepsilon)} - \frac{n(A \cap B)}{n(\varepsilon)}$$

$$\Rightarrow \quad P(A \text{ or } B) = P(A) + P(B) - P(A \text{ and } B)$$

5. (a), (c), (d), (e), (f) and (h) are identities.

2.2　Boolean algebra

> **(a)** Is $A \cap (B \cap C) = (A \cap B) \cap C$?
>
> **(b)** Is $A \cup (B \cup C) = (A \cup B) \cup C$?
>
> **(c)** What do your answers to (a) and (b) indicate about the operations of union and intersection ?

(a)　Yes　　　(b)　Yes

(c)　This indicates that the binary operations union and intersection are both **associative.**

> **Is addition distributive over multiplication?**

$1 + (1 \times 1) \neq (1 + 1) \times (1 + 1)$

Addition is therefore **not** distributive over multiplication.

> **Is intersection distributive over union:**
> is $A \cap (B \cup C) = (A \cap B) \cup (A \cap C)$?

Yes, both the left-hand side and the right-hand side are represented by the shaded area shown below on the Venn diagram.

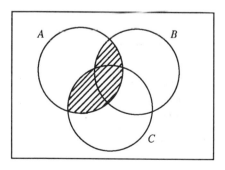

> Since $(A \cup B')' \cap B = A' \cap B$, does it follow that $(A \cup B')' = A'$?

It does **not** follow that $(A \cup B')' = A'$. This is clear from a Venn diagram.

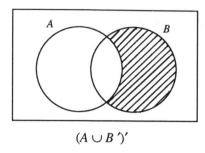

$(A \cup B')'$

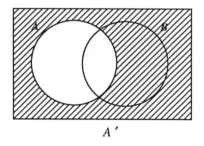

A'

It is important to note that whereas, in ordinary algebra, $ax = bx \Rightarrow a = b$, the equivalent result is **not** true for set algebra:

If $A \cap X = B \cap X$ then it does **not** follow that $A = B$. A simple example is

$A = \{1, 2\}$, $B = \{2, 3\}$ and $X = \{2\}$. Then $A \cap X = B \cap X$, but $A \neq B$.

Exercise 2

1. (a) $A \cap (A' \cup B)$ (b) $(A \cup B)' \cap \varnothing$

    (c) $(A' \cap \varepsilon) \cup (A \cap \varnothing)$

2. The diagram is the same for both (a) and (b).

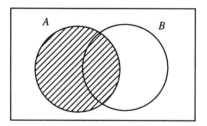

This shows that $A \cup (A \cap B) = A$ and $A \cap (A \cup B) = A$

108

3. (a) $A \cup (A \cap B) = (A \cap \varepsilon) \cup (A \cap B)$ *identity law*
$$= A \cap (\varepsilon \cup B) \quad \text{\textit{distributive law}}$$
$$= A \cap \varepsilon \quad\quad\quad \text{\textit{identity law}}$$
$$= A \quad\quad\quad\quad \text{\textit{identity law}}$$

(b) $A \cap (A \cup B) = (A \cup \varnothing) \cap (A \cup B)$
$$= A \cup (\varnothing \cap B)$$
$$= A \cup \varnothing$$
$$= A$$

4 (a) 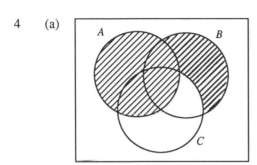 (b)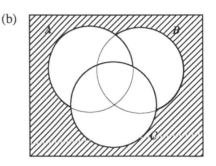

(c)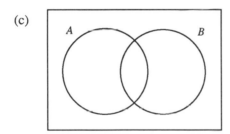

5. (a) $(A \cup B') \cap (A \cup B) = A \cup (B' \cap B)$ *distributive law*
$$= A \cup \varnothing \quad\quad \text{\textit{complement law}}$$
$$= A \quad\quad\quad\quad \text{\textit{identity law}}$$

(b) $(A \cup B') \cap (A \cup B) = A$ *proved above*
$$\Rightarrow (A \cap B') \cup (A \cap B) = A \quad \text{\textit{principle of duality}}$$

(c) $A \cup (A \cup B')' = A \cup (A' \cap (B')')$ *de Morgan's law*
$$= A \cup (A' \cap B) \quad\quad\quad \text{\textit{complement law}}$$
$$= (A \cup A') \cap (A \cup B) \quad \text{\textit{distributive law}}$$
$$= \varepsilon \cap (A \cup B) \quad\quad\quad\quad \text{\textit{complement law}}$$
$$= A \cup B \quad\quad\quad\quad\quad\quad\quad \text{\textit{identity law}}$$

2.3 Switching circuits

> **Design a 'stairway' circuit with 2 two-way switches, *A* and *B*, and a single light fitting**

The simplest design is

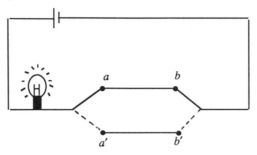

Such an arrangement will allow current to flow if either both the switches are 'up' of if both the switches are 'down'. The circuit can be broken (i.e. the light can be switched off) by changing the position of either switch.

It is conventional to represent such a circuit in a simplified diagram which shows the position of the switch which allows current to flow.

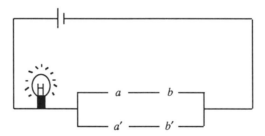

> **What Boolean expression represents this arrangement?**

Current will flow if the switches are in any one of the three positions shown in the Venn diagram.

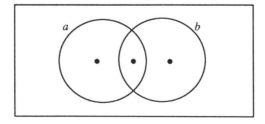

The Boolean expression for this arrangement is therefore $a \cup b$.

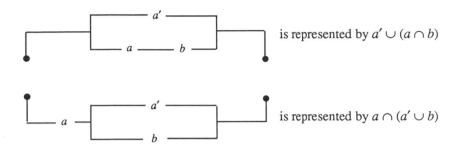

What is the Boolean expression which represents this circuit?

is represented by $a' \cup (a \cap b)$

is represented by $a \cap (a' \cup b)$

so the complete circuit is represented by

$$(a' \cup (a \cap b)) \cup (a \cap (a' \cup b))$$

Exercise 3

1. (a)

    (b) $(a \cup b) \cap (a \cup c) = a \cup (b \cap c)$

    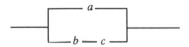

2. $\varepsilon \cup a = \varepsilon$

    The universal set represents all the possible settings of the switches in a circuit. If current flows regardless of the way the switches are set, then the switches are redundant and •——ε——• is the same as •———• Similarly, •— $\varnothing$ —• is the same as •———• •———• (the circuit is permanently broken).

3. $a \cup (a \cap b) = a$ is illustrated by

    $= \bullet\!-\!a\!-\!\bullet$

    $a \cap (a \cup b) = a$ is illustrated by

    $= \bullet\!-\!a\!-\!\bullet$

111

4. Applying the distributive law to the first circuit,

$$(x \cap (y \cup z)) \cup (y \cap z) = ((x \cap y) \cup (x \cap z)) \cup (y \cap z)$$

Applying the distributive law to the second circuit,

$$(x \cap y) \cup (z \cap (x \cup y)) = (x \cap y) \cup ((z \cap x) \cup (z \cap y))$$

The first can be shown to be equivalent to the second by applying the commutative law, giving

$$((x \cap y) \cup (z \cap x)) \cup (z \cap y)$$

and then applying the associative law, giving

$$(x \cap y) \cup ((z \cap x)) \cup (z \cap y))$$

5E. The top part of the circuit,

is represented by

$a \cap ((b \cap a') \cup (c \cap a))$

$=$	$(a \cap (b \cap a')) \cup (a \cap (c \cap a))$	*the distributive law*
$=$	$((a \cap a') \cap b) \cup ((a \cap a) \cap c)$	*the commutative and associative laws*
$=$	$(\emptyset \cap b) \cup (a \cap c)$	*the complement and idempotent laws*
$=$	$\emptyset \cup (a \cap c)$	*the identity law*
$=$	$a \cap c$	*the identity law*

giving an equivalent circuit

The bottom part of the circuit is represented by

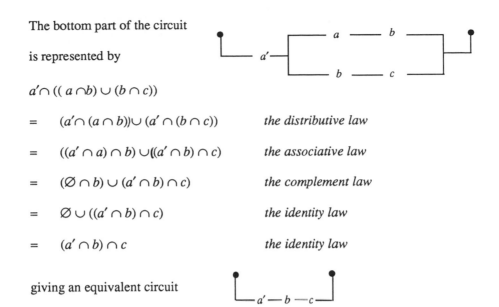

$a' \cap ((a \cap b) \cup (b \cap c))$

$=$	$(a' \cap (a \cap b)) \cup (a' \cap (b \cap c))$	*the distributive law*
$=$	$((a' \cap a) \cap b) \cup ((a' \cap b) \cap c)$	*the associative law*
$=$	$(\emptyset \cap b) \cup (a' \cap b) \cap c)$	*the complement law*
$=$	$\emptyset \cup ((a' \cap b) \cap c)$	*the identity law*
$=$	$(a' \cap b) \cap c$	*the identity law*

giving an equivalent circuit

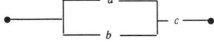

The complete circuit is now reduced to

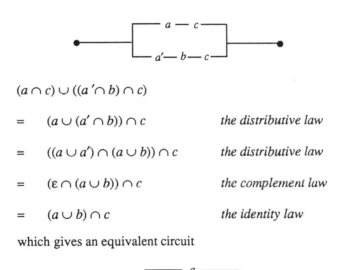

$(a \cap c) \cup ((a' \cap b) \cap c)$

$=$	$(a \cup (a' \cap b)) \cap c$	*the distributive law*
$=$	$((a \cup a') \cap (a \cup b)) \cap c$	*the distributive law*
$=$	$(\varepsilon \cap (a \cup b)) \cap c$	*the complement law*
$=$	$(a \cup b) \cap c$	*the identity law*

which gives an equivalent circuit

2.4   Sets of numbers

> **Why is it not possible to measure the length of the line precisely?**

The length of a line might be 0.05m to 2 decimal places, 0.054m to 3 decimal places, 0.0538m to 4 decimal places and so on. The measurement will depend upon the accuracy of the measuring device.

> **Is 3.14 rational number? is $0.\dot{1}$ rational?**

$3.14 = \frac{314}{100}$ and $0.\dot{1} = \frac{1}{9}$, so both these numbers are rational.

All decimals which terminate or recur are rational.

> **(a)** Draw a Venn diagram to show the relationship between these sets.
>
> **(b)** Use set notation to describe the set of irrational numbers in terms of $\mathbb{Q}$ and $\mathbb{R}$.

(a)

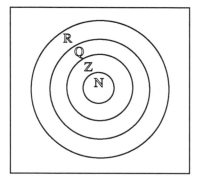

(b)　The set of irrational numbers is shown as the shaded set in the diagram:

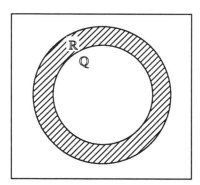

The irrational numbers are the set $\mathbb{R} \cap \mathbb{Q}'$.

> **Set M is defined as the 'the set of all non-$\mathfrak{R}$ sets'.**
> **Is M an $\mathfrak{R}$ set or is it a non-$\mathfrak{R}$ set?**

If M is an $\mathfrak{R}$ set then it must contain itself as an element. However, this is not possible as the elements of M are all non-$\mathfrak{R}$ sets, so M is **not** an $\mathfrak{R}$ set.

If M is a non-$\mathfrak{R}$ set then it **must** contain itself because M is the set of **all** non-$\mathfrak{R}$ sets. Thus it must be an $\mathfrak{R}$ set, which is a contradiction.

This is 'Russell's paradox'.

2.5　Infinity

(a)　The new set will also have cardinality $\aleph_0$.

For example,

the set $\{1,3,5,7, \dots \}$　　has cardinality $\aleph_0$,

the set $\{2,4,6,8, \dots \}$　　has cardinality $\aleph_0$,

and the combined set $\{1,2,3,4,5,6,7,8, \dots \}$ also has cardinality $\aleph_0$.

(b)　This shows that $\aleph_0 + \aleph_0 = \aleph_0$.

Yes.

The number $\dfrac{49}{313}$ would be included in the diagonal when the sum of the numerator and the denominator is 362. It will therefore be in the sequence

$$\frac{361}{1}, \ \frac{360}{2}, \ \frac{359}{3}, \ \dots \ \frac{3}{359}, \ \frac{2}{360}, \ \frac{1}{361},$$

Similarly $\dfrac{3594}{13}$ will be in the sequence when the sum of the denominator and the numerator is 3607 and will be found in the sequence

$$\frac{1}{3606}, \ \frac{2}{3605}, \ \dots \ , \ \frac{3605}{2}, \ \frac{3606}{1}$$

Notice that the same number will occur more than once in the list. However, this does not invalidate the argument that the set is countable.

3 Group theory

3.1 Symmetry

> With reference to the above examples, decide what it means to say that something exhibits 'symmetry'. Can you find a general definition which applies to all three of the above examples?

The first picture exhibits reflection symmetry. It is **unchanged** when reflected in a centrally placed vertical line.

The polynomial is **unchanged** under a transformation which interchanges the coefficients of 1 and x^4 and of x and x^3.

You may have simply said that the Chinese figure is **unchanged** when rotated 180° about its centre. In fact it has to be transformed by the rotation **and** the interchange of black and white.

[For followers of the Chinese **Tao**, living in harmony with nature involves balancing opposing tendencies of various types. The rotational symmetry of the dark **yin** and the light **yang** symbolises the cyclic nature of change. Furthermore, where each force is at a maximum, there is the seed of its opposite.]

The common feature of all the examples is that there is a **transformation** under which the object is unchanged:

- a reflection;
- $x^a \rightarrow x^{4-a}$;
- a 180° rotation and the interchange of black-white.

> Without using any laws of mechanics, explain why you would expect y to equal x. Explain why $v = \frac{u}{2} - x$ and $w = y + \frac{u}{2}$ and hence find $mv + mw$. State what law your reasoning has 'discovered'.

Since the collision is symmetrical, you would expect $y = x$.

The velocities $\xrightarrow{\ v\ }$ and $\xrightarrow{\ w\ }$ are observed as $\xrightarrow{\ v - \frac{u}{2}\ }$ and $\xrightarrow{\ w - \frac{u}{2}\ }$

Thus $v - \frac{u}{2} = -x$ and $w - \frac{u}{2} = y$. Therefore $v = \frac{u}{2} - x$, $w = \frac{u}{2} + y$.

Then $v + w = u$ and $mv + mw$ is equal to mu .

You have discovered the Law of Conservation of Momentum.

3.2 Transformations

> **For the 4 x 5 board shown below:**
>
> **find which row and column flips can be used to transform pattern A into pattern B;**
>
> **find which can be used to transform B into A;**
>
> **think of a notation that would help you to describe your transformations.**

You may have noticed that the **same** transformation which changes pattern A into pattern B also transforms B back into A.

A possible notation would be to use R_i to denote flipping the ith row and C_i to denote flipping the ith column. Then the required transformation is to flip rows 2 and 4, then columns 1 and 4. This could be written as $C_4 C_1 R_4 R_2$.

You may also have noticed that the order in which the flips are performed does **not** matter. For example, the transformation $C_4 C_1 R_4 R_2$ could have been written as $C_1 R_2 C_4 R_4$ or $R_4 R_2 C_4 C_1$ or with **any** other ordering of the symbols. The combination of these flips is **commutative**.

You might have found another set of row and column flips which could have been used:

$$C_5 C_3 C_2 R_3 R_1.$$

This idea is considered further in the commentary to the discussion point.

3.3 Symmetry groups

> **Complete the above list of symmetries**

A clockwise rotation of 240° : S
A clockwise rotation of 360° : I
A reflection in line n : N

> **What symmetry would R^3 represent?**

R^3 represents a clockwise rotation of 360°, i.e. the identity transformation.

> **What does R (ST) mean?**

R (ST) means **R** after **(ST)**   i.e. **R** after **S** after **T**

Exercise 1

1. There are 4 symmetries

    The identity element : **I**
    A reflection in the x-axis : **X**
    A reflection in the y-axis : **Y**
    A rotation of 180° : **R**

	I	X	Y	R
I	I	X	Y	R
X	X	I	R	Y
Y	Y	R	I	X
R	R	Y	X	I

    The table exhibits closure.
    All elements are self-inverse.

2. There are 8 symmetries

    The identity element : **I**
    A rotation of 90° : **R**
    A rotation of 180° : **R²**
    A rotation of 270° : **R³**
    A reflection in the x-axis : **X**
    A reflection in the y-axis : **Y**
    A reflection in diagonal m : **M**
    A reflection in diagonal n : **N**

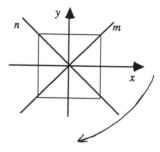

	I	R	R²	R³	X	N	Y	M
I	I	R	R²	R³	X	N	Y	M
R	R	R²	R³	I	N	Y	M	X
R²	R²	R³	I	R	Y	M	X	N
R³	R³	I	R	R²	M	X	N	Y
X	X	M	Y	N	I	R³	R²	R
N	N	X	M	Y	R	I	R³	R²
Y	Y	N	X	M	R²	R	I	R³
M	M	Y	N	X	R³	R²	R	I

The complete table is not necessary to answer the question. However, the fact that it is not symmetric about the main diagonal shows that the combination of symmetries is not commutative.

3E. 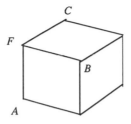   If vertex F is fixed, then the symmetries simply permute the vertices A, B and C.

There are three 'physically possible' symmetries:

•   the identity transformation;

•   a rotation of $120°$ about the space diagonal through F;

•   a rotation of $240°$ about the space diagonal through F.

There are also three other symmetries:

•   a reflection in the diagonal plane through FA;

•   a reflection in the diagonal plane through FB;

•   a reflection in the diagonal plane through FC.

The symmetries act as symmetries of the triangle ABC.

3.4   Groups

> **Which of the following sets of numbers form groups? Justify your answers.**
>
> **(a)   All integers under subtraction.**
> **(b)   {1,10} under multiplication modulo 11.**
> **(c)   All irrational numbers under multiplication.**

(a)   This is not a group because subtraction is not associative.

(b)

$\times_{11}$	1	10
1	1	10
10	10	1

This forms a group - all the properties are satisfied
(N.B. $10 \times 10 = 9 \times 11 + 1$)

(c)   This is not a group - there is no identity.

119

$$\begin{array}{llll}
 & ba & = & ca \\
\Rightarrow & (ba)a^{-1} & = & (ca)\,a^{-1} & \text{post multiply by } a^{-1} \\
\Rightarrow & b\,(aa^{-1}) & = & c\,(aa^{-1}) & \text{associativity} \\
\Rightarrow & b\,e & = & c\,e & \text{inverse} \\
\Rightarrow & b & = & c & \text{identity}
\end{array}$$

Exercise 2

1. (a) Does not possess the latin square property.

   (b)

	a	b	c	d
a	b	d	a	c
b	d	c	b	a
c	a	b	c	d
d	c	a	d	b

   can be rearranged as

	c	a	b	d
c	c	a	b	d
a	a	b	d	c
b	b	d	c	a
d	d	c	a	b

   The rearranged table has the cyclic group property and is isomorphic to $\mathbb{Z}_4$.

2. (a) Yes. All the properties are satisfied with 0 the identity.

   (b) No. It is not closed and there is no identity.

   (c) Yes. All group properties hold.

3.

x_7	1	2	3	4	5	6
1	1	2	3	4	5	6
2	2	4	6	1	3	5
3	3	6	2	5	1	4
4	4	1	5	2	6	3
5	5	3	1	6	4	2
6	6	5	4	3	2	1

   From the table:

   - closure is clear;

   - 1 is the identity element;

   - all elements have inverses since 1 appears in every row and column, symmetrically arranged about the main diagonal.

4. From the group table as given on Tasksheet 1,

$$L^{-1} = L$$
$$M^{-1} = M$$
$$N^{-1} = N$$
$$R^{-1} = R^2$$

$\left.\right\}$ Self-inverse

5. Elements which are not self-inverse can be paired off with their inverses. There are therefore an even number of self-inverse elements.

Since the identity element is self-inverse, there is at least one other self-inverse element.

3.5 Subgroups

Exercise 3

1. (a)

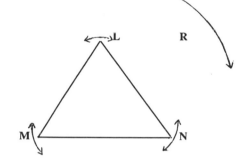

	I	R	R²	L	M	N
I	I	R	R²	L	M	N
R	R	R²	I	M	N	L
R²	R²	I	R	N	L	M
L	L	N	M	I	R²	R
M	M	L	N	R	I	R²
N	N	M	L	R²	R	I

$I : I, I^2 = I$	I generates $\{ I \}$
$R : R, R^2, R^3 = I$	R generates $\{ I, R, R^2 \}$
$R^2 : R^2, R^4 = R, R^6 = I$	R^2 generates $\{ I, R, R^2 \}$
$L : L, L^2 = I$	L generates $\{ I, L \}$
$M : M, M^2 = I$	M generates $\{ I, M \}$
$N : N, N^2 = I$	N generates $\{ I, N \}$

(b) No element generates the whole group and so the group is not cyclic.

2. (a) 1 generates $\{ 1 \}$
   2 generates $\{ 2, 4, 1 \}$ $\quad = \{ 1, 2, 4 \}$
   3 generates $\{ 3, 2, 6, 4, 5, 1 \} = \{ 1, 2, 3, 4, 5, 6 \}$
   4 generates $\{ 4, 2, 1 \}$ $\quad = \{ 1, 2, 4 \}$
   5 generates $\{ 5, 4, 6, 2, 3, 1 \} = \{ 1, 2, 3, 4, 5, 6 \}$
   6 generates $\{ 6, 1 \}$ $\quad = \{ 1, 6 \}$

(b) This is a cyclic group because it has elements which generate the whole group.

3. 6 is the identity element viz $2 \times 6 = 12 \equiv 2 \,(\text{mod } 10)$

$$4 \times 6 = 24 \equiv 4 \,(\text{mod } 10) \quad \text{etc.}$$

The subgroups are $\{\, 6 \,\}$, $\{\, 6, 4, \,\}$, $\{\, 6, 2, 4, 8 \,\}$.

4. (a) The elements a and a^3 generate the group.

(b) (i)   For $\{\, e, a, a^2, a^3, a^4 \,\}$, all elements other than e generate the group.

(ii) For $\{\, e, a, a^2, a^3, a^4, a^5 \,\}$, the elements a and a^5 generate the group.

(iii) For $\{\, e, a, a^2, \dots, a^{20} \,\}$, a^n generates the group if n is 1, 3, 7, 9, 11, 13, 17 or 19 i.e. if n has no factors in common with 20.

5. $aa^{-1} = a^{-1}a = e$ and so the elements a and a^{-1} commute with each other. For any power n,

$$e = (aa^{-1})^n$$

$$= (aa^{-1})(aa^{-1}) \dots (aa^{-1})$$

$$= a^n (a^{-1})^n, \quad \text{using associativity and commutativity}$$

Then $a^n = e$ if and only if $(a^{-1})^n = e$, a and a^{-1} therefore have the same order.

3.6   Lagrange's Theorem

> **List some of the things you notice about this 'cut-down' group table.**

One thing you may have noticed is that the pattern of the $\{\, \mathbf{I}, \mathbf{R}, \mathbf{R}^2 \,\}$ sub-table is repeated in the last 3 columns:

α	β	γ
β	γ	α
γ	α	β

> **Explain how Lagrange's Theorem follows from the result about patterns of elements.**

The first $|\,H\,|$ rows of the table must form into a whole number of $|\,H\,| \times |\,H\,|$ squares. This is only possible if $|\,H\,|$ divides $|\,G\,|$.

Exercise 4

1. A reflection has order 2, so $M^2 = I$
    A rotation of 90° has order 4, so $R^4 = I$

    The order of the group must be a multiple of 4 by Lagrange's Theorem, since it contains a cyclic subgroup of order 4. The order cannot be 4 since **M** is not an element of the cyclic subgroup.

    The smallest order is thus 8, and the group could be the symmetries of a square.

2. (a) $\{a, b\}$ is a group because it is essentially the same as the group $\{0, 1\}$ of integers under addition modulo 2.

    If the set of 5 elements were a group, then Lagrange's Theorem would imply that 2 is a factor of 5. The 5 elements therefore do **not** form a group.

    [This is an example of a type of proof called proof by contradiction which you will study in Chapter 4]

    (b) It is clear from the table that the set is closed, that a is the identity element and that each element is self-inverse. It must therefore be associativity which is **not** satisfied! For example:

    $$(bc)d = ed = b$$
    $$b(cd) = be = d$$

3. The group of a symmetries of a square has order 8. By Lagrange's Theorem, it can only have subgroups of orders 1, 2, 4 and 8.

    Using the notation from Tasksheet 4:

    Orders 1 and 8

    These subgroups are simply $\{I\}$ and the whole group.

    Order 2

    Each such subgroup must consist of the identity and one self-inverse element,

    $\{I, R^2\}$, $\{I, A\}$, $\{I, L\}$, $\{I, B\}$, $\{I, M\}$.

    Order 4

    If such a subgroup contained an element of order 4 then it would be $\{I, R, R^2, R^3\}$. Otherwise it would contain the identity element and three elements of order 2.

    The only such sets which are closed are the subgroups $\{I, R^2, A, B\}$ and $\{I, R^2, L, M\}$.

123

4. A subgroup other than the whole group must have order 1, 2 or 3. If the order is 1 there is nothing to prove.

    Any non-identity element of the subgroup generates a cyclic subgroup. This must itself have order 2 or 3 and must therefore be the whole of the original subgroup.

5. (a) a^3 has order 3 because $a^3 \neq e$, $(a^3)^2 = a^6 \neq e$ and $(a^3)^3 = a^9 = e$.

    (b) Let a be any non-identity element. By Lagrange's Theorem, a has order 3 or 9. If a has order 3 then $\{e, a, a^2\}$ is the required subgroup whereas if a has order 9 then $\{e, a^3, a^6\}$ is the required subgroup.

    (c) Let a be any non-identity element, then a has order 3, 9 or 27. The required subgroup is then $\{e, a, a^2\}$, $\{e, a^3, a^6\}$ or $\{e, a^9, a^{18}\}$, respectively.

3.7   Applications of Lagrange's Theorem

> **What does Fermat's Little Theorem claim in the case when $a = 4$ and $p = 3$? Check the result in this case and one other case of your own choosing.**

The claim is that $(4^3 - 4)$ is divisible by 3.

This is true since $4^3 - 4 = 3 \times 20$.

You should find the result to be true for any case of your own choosing.

Exercise 5

1. If the elements are **I**, **R**, **M** and **N**, then $\mathbf{R}^2 = \mathbf{M}^2 = \mathbf{N}^2 = \mathbf{I}$ and no element generates the group; therefore K is not a cyclic group.

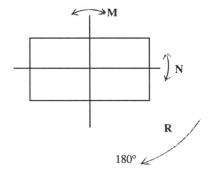

2. By Lagrange's Theorem, each subgroup of a group of order 4 has order 1, 2 or 4.

    Any element of the group generates a cyclic subgroup and must therefore also have order 1, 2 or 4.

3. (a) The group is non-cyclic, so there is no element of order 4.

Thus all non-identity elements are of order 2 and are self-inverse. The table is therefore of the form given.

(b) a and e are already in row a and b is already in column b. Therefore $ab \neq a$, e or b and so $ab = c$.

It is now easy to use the Latin Square property to complete the table.

	e	a	b	c
e	e	a	b	c
a	a	e	c	b
b	b	c	e	a
c	c	b	a	e

The Latin Square property allows no other possibility.

3.8 Isomorphic groups

> **Explain why there are no other groups with 1, 2, 3, 5 or 7 elements.**

2, 3, 5 and 7 are prime numbers and so, by Lagrange's Theorem, groups of these orders have no subgroups. Then any non-identity element generates the whole group and so the group is cyclic.

Exercise 6

1. (a) K because all elements are self-inverse.

(b) Z_4 because it is cyclic, generated by 2 or 8.

(c) K because all elements are self-inverse.

(d) Z_4 because it is cyclic, generated by $\pm j$.

2. (a) There are 12 elements.

- Six rotations $\mathbf{R}$, $\mathbf{R}^2$, $\mathbf{R}^3$, $\mathbf{R}^4$, $\mathbf{R}^5$ and $\mathbf{I}$, where $\mathbf{R}$ is a rotation of $60°$.

- Three reflections in lines joining opposite vertices.

- Three reflections in lines joining midpoint of opposite edges.

(b) **Order 1** - $\{\mathbf{I}\}$

Order 2 - There are 7 subgroups of order 2, each formed by $\mathbf{I}$ and an element of order 2 i.e. $\mathbf{R}^3$ or one of the reflections.

Order 3 - A subgroup of order 3 must contain an element of order 3. There is therefore only $\{\mathbf{I}, \mathbf{R}^2, \mathbf{R}^4\}$.

Order 4 - There is no element of order 4 and so all subgroups of order 4 are isomorphic to K. In particular, they contain self-inverse elements which commute with each other.

There are 3 such subgroups, each consisting of $\mathbf{I}$, $\mathbf{R}^3$ and a pair of reflections at right-angles to each other.

It is interesting to note that the combination of any two reflections is always a rotation.

Order 6 - A cyclic subgroup of order 6 must contain an element of order 6 and so the only such subgroup is the group of six rotations.

All other subgroups of order 6 must be isomorphic to S_3. They therefore contain a subgroup of order 3 i.e. $\{\mathbf{I}, \mathbf{R}^2, \mathbf{R}^4\}$.

There are two such subgroups, each consisting of $\mathbf{I}$, $\mathbf{R}^2$, $\mathbf{R}^4$ and three reflections at $120°$ to each other.

Order 12 - The only subgroup of order 12 is the original group itself.

4 *Mathematical proof*

4.2 Direct proof

> **Explain how you know that the last digit of $100k^2$ is 0. Complete the above proof. Can you find any ways to simplify your proof?**

For any integer a, the decimal representation of $10a$ can be obtained simply by adding a final 0 to the decimal representation of a. $100k^2$ is equal to $10 \times 10 \times k^2$ and therefore ends in two zeros.

The proof might continue:

If $n = 10k + 1$, then $n^2 = 100k^2 + 20k + 1$ has last digit 1,

If $n = 10k + 2$, then $n^2 = 100k^2 + 40k + 4$ has last digit 4, etc.

The proof can be made much shorter (but perhaps not simpler!) by using more algebra. For example:

Let $n = 10k + a$ where $a \in \{0,1,2,3,4,5,6,7,8,9\}$ then $n^2 = 100 \times k^2 + 10 \times 2ak + a^2$.

Therefore, n^2 has the same last digit as $a^2 \in \{0,1,4,9,16,25,36,49,64,81\}$ and cannot end in 2,3,7 or 8.

> **Extend the above proof to numbers with three digits.**

Let N have 100's digit a, 10's digit b and units digit c.

The sum of N's digits is $a + b + c$ and so you can assume that $a + b + c = 3M$, where M is an integer.

$$\begin{aligned} \text{Then } N &= 100a + 10b + c \\ &= 99a + 9b + (a + b + c) \\ &= 3(33a + 3b + M) \end{aligned}$$

N therefore has a factor of 3.

Exercise 1

1. (a) $2n = 2 \times n$ has a factor of 2 and is therefore an even number.

    (b) There are many possible answers, for example $2n - 1$ or $2n + 1$.

    (c) Let the odd numbers be $2n + 1$ and $2m + 1$.

    Then $(2n + 1) + (2m + 1) = 2n + 2m + 2$

    $$= 2(n + m + 1), \text{ an even number.}$$

    (d) Let the odd numbers be $2n + 1$ and $2m + 1$.

    Then $(2m + 1)(2n + 1) = 4mn + 2m + 2n + 1$

    $$= 2[2mn + m + n] + 1, \text{ an odd number.}$$

2. A good rule is **'the number is divisible by 9 if and only if the sum of its digits is divisible by 9'**.

    The following proof is for 3 digit numbers. Let N have 100's digit a, 10's digit b and units digit c.

    Then $N = 100a + 10b + c$

    $\qquad = 99a + 9b + a + b + c$

    $\qquad = 9(11a + b) + (a + b + c)$

    Then N is divisible by 9 if and only if $a + b + c$ is divisible by 9.

3. (a) You will find that the rule always works although you will sometimes need to make 'carries'.

    E.g.
    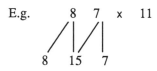

    The product is 957

(b) The rule gives

$$a \quad a+b \quad b$$

This agrees with the algebraic multiplication:

$$(10a + b) \times 11 = 110a + 11b$$

$$= 100a + 10a + 10b + b$$

$$= 100a + 10(a + b) + b$$

4. (a) The diagonal difference is always 14

(b) The general 2 x 2 square is

n	$n + 2$
$n + 7$	$n + 9$

The general diagonal difference is therefore

$$(n + 2)(n + 7) - n(n + 9) = n^2 + 9n + 14 - n^2 - 9n$$

$$= 14.$$

5E. (a) $3^2 + 4^2 = 25 = 5^2$

$5^2 + 12^2 = 169 = 13^2$

$7^2 + 24^2 = 625 = 25^2$

$9^2 + 40^2 = 1681 = 41^2$

(b) (11, 60, 61) and (13, 84, 85) similarly satisfy Pythagoras' theorem.

(c) $2r + 1$

(d)

r	1	2	3	4	...
$2r(r + 1)$	4	12	24	40	...

(e) $(2r + 1, \ 2r(r + 1), \ 2r(r + 1) + 1)$

(f) $(2r(r + 1) + 1)^2 = (2r(r + 1))^2 + 2 \times 2r(r + 1) + 1$

$$= (2r(r + 1))^2 + 4r^2 + 4r + 1$$

$$= (2r(r + 1))^2 + (2r + 1)^2$$

The rth triple therefore satisfies Pythagoras' theorem.

4.3   Axiomatic proof

> Conversely, show that $x = a^{-1}b \Rightarrow ax = b$

$$x = a^{-1}b$$

$\Rightarrow ax = a(a^{-1}b)$ (closure)

$\Rightarrow ax = (aa^{-1})b$ (associativity)

$\Rightarrow ax = eb$ (inverse property)

$\Rightarrow ax = b$ (identity)

> **Use this result to show that the sum of the interior angles of a quadrilateral is 360°.**

Join a pair of opposite vertices of the quadrilateral to form two triangles.   [1]

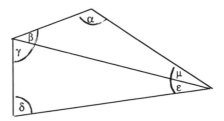

$$\alpha + (\beta + \gamma) + \delta + (\varepsilon + \mu) = (\alpha + \beta + \mu) + (\gamma + \delta + \varepsilon) \qquad [2]$$
$$= 180° + 180°$$
$$= 360°$$

[1]   The fact that such a construction can be made does itself require proof. For example, you cannot choose **any** pair of opposite vertices in the quadrilateral:

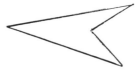

[2]   This step requires the associativity and commutativity of addition.

Exercise 2

1.

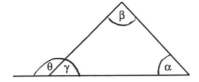

$\alpha + \beta + \gamma = 180°$ (Angle sum of triangle)

Also, $\theta + \gamma = 180°$ (Result 1)

So $\theta = \alpha + \beta$

2.   (a)   Draw the diameter AD through the point A at the circumference.

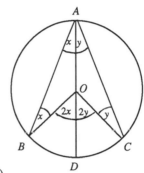

$AO = BO$ (radii of a circle)

$\Rightarrow \angle BAO = \angle ABO$ ($\triangle AOB$ is isosceles)

Let these angles be x, then

$\angle BOD = \angle BAO + \angle ABO$ (Exterior angle result)

$= 2x$

Similarly, $\angle CAO = \angle ACO = y$ and $\angle COD = 2y$

Then $\beta = 2x + 2y$

$= 2(x + y)$ (Distributive law)

$= 2\alpha$

(b)   All the radii of a circle are equal in length.

If two sides of a triangle are equal in length then the angles opposite these two sides are also equal.

The exterior angle of a triangle is equal to the sum of the opposite two interior angles.

Multiplication is distributive over addition.

3. (a) $a^2b = (aa) b$

   $= a (ab)$ (associativity)

   $= a (ba)$ $(ab = ba)$

   $= (ab) a$ (associativity)

   $= (ba) a$ $(ab = ba)$

   $= b (aa)$ (associativity)

   $= ba^2$

   (b) $eb = be$ (identity)

   $\Rightarrow (aa^{-1}) b = b (aa^{-1})$ (inverse property)

   $\Rightarrow a (a^{-1}b) = (ba) a^{-1}$ (associativity)

   $\Rightarrow a (a^{-1}b) = (ab) a^{-1}$ $(ba = ab)$

   $\Rightarrow a (a^{-1}b) = a (ba^{-1})$ (associativity)

   $\Rightarrow \quad a^{-1}b = ba^{-1}$ (cancellation laws)

4. $(b^{-1}a^{-1})(ab) = b^{-1} (a^{-1} (ab))$ (associativity)

   $= b^{-1} ((a^{-1}a) b)$ (associativity)

   $= b^{-1} (eb)$ (inverse property)

   $= b^{-1}b$ (identity)

   $= e$ (inverse property)

   Similarly, $(ab)(b^{-1}a^{-1}) = e$

   $b^{-1}a^{-1}$ and ab are therefore inverses of each other.

5. $A \cap \varnothing = A$ (given)

   but $A \cap \varnothing = \varnothing$ (identity)

   Therefore $A = \varnothing$

6.   (a)

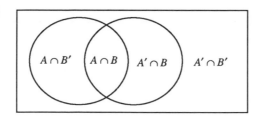

$(A \cap B) \cup (A \cap B') \cup (A' \cap B) \cup (A' \cap B') = \varepsilon$

(b) $(A \cap B) \cup (A \cap B') \cup (A' \cap B) \cup (A' \cap B')$

$$= ((A \cap B) \cup (A \cap B')) \cup ((A' \cap B) \cup (A' \cap B'))$$

$$= (A \cap (B \cup B')) \cup (A' \cap (B \cup B'))$$

$$= (A \cap \varepsilon) \cup (A' \cap \varepsilon)$$

$$= A \cup A'$$

$$= \varepsilon$$

4.4   Sequences of propositions

Prove that the following propositions are *not* true

(a) $2^n \leq n^3 + 1$ for $n \in \mathbb{N}$

(b) $n^2 + n + 41$ is prime for $n \in \mathbb{N}$

(c) $6^n + 4n^4$ is divisible by 5 for $n \in \mathbb{N}$

(d)   When n dots on the circumference of a circle are joined by straight lines, the maximum possible number of regions is 2^{n-1}.

(a)   P(10) is false.

In fact, P(1), P(2), ..., P(9) are all true.

(b)   P(41) is false because $41^2 + 41 + 41$ has a factor of 41. P(40) is also false because $40^2 + 40 + 41 = 41 \times 41$.

In fact, P(1), P(2), ..., P(39) are all true.

(c)   P(n) is false for $n = 5, 10, 15, \ldots$

(d)   P(6) is false. 6 dots produce at most 31 regions.

> (a) For the proposition
>
> $9^n + 7$ *is divisible by 8 for all natural numbers n*
>
> show that P(1), P(2), P(3) and P(4) are all true.
>
> (b) A computer could be programmed to check P(5), P(6), P(7) ... Explain why such a search cannot prove the original proposition.

(a)

$9^1 + 7$	=	16	=	2×8	:	P(1) is true
$9^2 + 7$	=	88	=	11×8	:	P(2) is true
$9^3 + 7$	=	736	=	92×8	:	P(3) is true
$9^4 + 7$	=	6568	=	821×8	:	P(4) is true

(b) Until you have proved the result to be generally true, you can never be **certain** that the next number will be divisible by 8. If you show that P(1), P(2), ... , P(999), P(1000) are all true but then stop, you will never know whether or not P(1001) is true.

As there is an inexhaustible supply of natural numbers, you can never prove this proposition by exhaustion.

> Find a proposition such that P(1), P(2), ... , P(10^6) are all true but such that P($10^6 + 1$) is false.

Perhaps the simplest such proposition is
  $n \leq 10^6$ for all natural numbers n.

4.5 Mathematical induction

> Explain why one of the above three cases must hold for any sequence of propositions.

If not all of the P(n) are true, then there is a first one which is false. This first one to be false is either P(1) or it is P($k + 1$), with P(1), P(2), ... , P(k) all true.

> Explain why it therefore follows that $h_{k+1} = h_k + k + 1$

Previously, there were h_k pieces. The ($k + 1$)th cut splits each of $k + 1$ regions into two pieces and so creates another $k + 1$ regions.

Therefore, $h_{k+1} = h_k + (k + 1)$.

Exercise 3

1. $P(1)$: $8^1 + 6$ is divisible by 14 is true. You must check if it is possible for $P(1), \ldots, P(k)$ to be true and yet $P(k + 1)$ false:

   Assume $P(k)$ is true : $\qquad 8^k + 6 = 14M$

   $$\text{Then} \quad 8^{k+1} + 6 \quad = \quad 8 \times 8^k + 6$$

   $$= \quad 8 \times (14M - 6) + 6$$

   $$= \quad 14 \times (8M - 3)$$

   Hence $P(k + 1)$ is true.

   By mathematical induction, the proposition is true for all natural numbers n.

2. $P(1)$: $1^3 - 1$ is a multiple of 3 is true. You must check if it is possible for $P(1), \ldots, P(k)$ to be true and yet $P(k + 1)$ false:

   Assume $P(k)$ is true : $\qquad k^3 - k = 3M$

   $$\text{Then} \quad (k + 1)^3 - (k + 1) = \quad k^3 + 3k^2 + 3k + 1 - k - 1$$

   $$= \quad k^3 - k + 3k^2 + 3k$$

   $$= \quad 3\,(M + k^2 + k)$$

   Hence $P(k + 1)$ is true.

   By mathematical induction, the proposition is true for all natural numbers n.

3. $P(1)$: $1 = \frac{1}{2}\,(1 + 1)$ is true. You must check if it is possible for $P(1), \ldots, P(k)$ to be true and yet $P(k + 1)$ false:

   Assume $P(k)$ is true : $\qquad 1 + 2 + \ldots + k \; = \frac{1}{2}k\,(k + 1)$

   $$\text{Then} \quad 1 + 2 + \ldots + k + (k + 1) \quad = \quad \frac{1}{2}\,k\,(k + 1) + (k + 1)$$

   $$= \quad (k + 1)\,(\tfrac{1}{2}k + 1)$$

   $$= \quad \frac{1}{2}\,(k + 1)\,(k + 2)$$

   Hence $P(k + 1)$ is true.

   By mathematical induction, the proposition is true for all natural numbers n.

4. $P(1) : 1^3 = \frac{1}{4} \times 2^2$ is true. You must check if it is possible for $P(1), \ldots, P(k)$ to be true and yet $P(k + 1)$ false:

Assume $P(k)$ is true : $\qquad 1^3 + 2^3 + \ldots + k^3 = \frac{k^2}{4}(k + 1)^2$

Then $\qquad 1^3 + 2^3 + \ldots + k^3 + (k + 1)^3 = \frac{k^2}{4}(k + 1)^2 + (k + 1)^3$

$$= \frac{(k+1)^2}{4}(k^2 + 4(k + 1))$$

$$= \frac{(k+1)^2}{4}(k^2 + 4k + 4)$$

$$= \frac{(k+1)^2}{4}(k + 2)^2$$

Hence $P(k + 1)$ is true.

By mathematical induction, the proposition is true for all natural numbers n.

5. $P(1) : \frac{1}{1 \times 2} = \frac{1}{1 + 1}$ is true. You must check if it is possible for $P(1), \ldots, P(k)$ to be true and yet $P(k + 1)$ false:

Assume $P(k)$ is true : $\frac{1}{1 \times 2} + \ldots + \frac{1}{k(k + 1)} = \frac{k}{k + 1}$

Then $\qquad \frac{1}{1 \times 2} + \ldots + \frac{1}{k(k + 1)} + \frac{1}{(k + 1)(k + 2)} = \frac{k}{k + 1} + \frac{1}{(k + 1)(k + 2)}$

$$= \frac{k(k + 2) + 1}{(k + 1)(k + 2)}$$

$$= \frac{(k + 1)^2}{(k + 1)(k + 2)}$$

$$= \frac{k + 1}{k + 2}$$

Hence $P(k + 1)$ is true.

By mathematical induction, the proposition is true for all natural numbers n.

6. $P(1) : 1^3 + 2^3 + 3^3$ is divisible by 9 i.e. 36 is divisible by 9 is true. You must check if it is possible for $P(1), \ldots, P(k)$ to be true and yet $P(k + 1)$ false:

Assume $P(k)$ is true : $k^3 + (k + 1)^3 + (k + 2)^3 = 9M$

Then $\qquad (k + 1)^3 + (k + 2)^3 + (k + 3)^3 = 9M - k^3 + (k + 3)^3$

$$= 9M - k^3 + k^3 + 9k^2 + 27k + 27$$

$$= 9(M + k^2 + 3k + 3)$$

Hence $P(k + 1)$ is true.

By mathematical induction, the proposition is true for all natural numbers n.

4.6   Proof by contradition

> **Explain why any odd number can be expressed in the form $2n + 1$.**

Any odd number is one more than an even number and is therefore one more than a multiple of 2. It can therefore be expressed as $2n + 1$.

> **Explain how you know that $4n(n + 1) + 1$ is odd.**

$4n(n + 1) + 1$ is odd because it is one more than the even number
$$4n(n + 1) = 2 \times 2n(n + 1).$$

> **Show that $\sqrt{5}$ is irrational. What happens when you attempt to prove $\sqrt{9}$ is irrational?**

Assume $\sqrt{5}$ is rational.

Then $\sqrt{5} = \dfrac{a}{b}$ (where a, b have **no** common factor)

$\Rightarrow \quad 5 = \dfrac{a^2}{b^2}$

$\Rightarrow \quad 5b^2 = a^2$

So a^2 has a factor of 5. By a method similar to that of Example 7, it is easy to show that a therefore has a factor of 5.

Let $a = 5k$

Then $a^2 = 25k^2$

$\Rightarrow 5b^2 = 25k^2$

$\Rightarrow b^2 = 5k^2$

$\Rightarrow b$ has a factor of 5.

a and b therefore have a common factor of 5.

This **contradicts** the initial assumption that a and b have **no** common factor. Hence $\sqrt{5}$ cannot be a rational number.

When you use $\sqrt{9}$, you find that
$$\sqrt{9} = \frac{a}{b}$$

$\Rightarrow \quad 9b^2 = a^2$

$\Rightarrow \quad 3b = \pm a$

Instead of a contradiction, you obtain the correct result that $\sqrt{9} = 3$.

4.7   Mathematics and computers

> **(a)**   Show that $\pi(10) = 4$.
>
> **(b)**   Find the 168th prime number.
>
> **(c)**   Use a calculator or short program and the above table of values of $\pi(N)$ to check the Prime Number Theorem.

(a)   The first few primes are 2, 3, 5, 7, 11, 13, 17, 19, 23, 29, 31, 37, ...   Precisely 4 of these are less than 10.

(b) $\pi(1000) = 168$ and so the 168th prime is the largest prime less than 1000. Of the numbers ... 996, 997, 998 and 999, only 997 is not divisible by 2 or 3. You can easily check that it is also not divisible by any of the other primes less than $\sqrt{997}$. 997 is therefore the 168th prime.

(c) $\dfrac{10}{\ln 10} \approx 4.3$, $\dfrac{100}{\ln 100} \approx 21.7$, ... , $\dfrac{10^{10}}{\ln(10^{10})} \approx 434294482$.

In each case you will find that $\dfrac{N}{\ln N}$ is a good estimate for $\pi(N)$.

> **(a)**   Find a four colouring of the South American map shown above, treating the sea as a 'country'.
>
> **(b)**   Find a map drawn on a torus (a ring doughnut) which requires 5 colours.

(a)   Change the 'colouring' of Venezuela to dots, interchange the colouring of Argentine and Bolivia and then 'colour' the sea with x's.

(b)   There is a simple solution with just five regions:

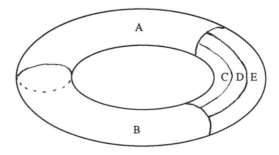

C and E meet each other on the underside of the torus.

This is an example of 'proof by contradiction'. When developing such a proof, mathematicians often consider a **minimal counterexample**. They then try to discover more and more about the minimal counterexample until they obtain a contradiction.

For Kempe's proof, a counterexample is a map which cannot be four coloured. A minimal counterexample is a counterexample with the smallest possible number of countries.

As an example of how mathematicians discover more about minimal counterexamples, consider how Kempe proved that a four colouring minimal counterexample has no country adjacent to only four other countries:

Suppose the counterexample has a country adjacent to only four other countries. This map can then be reduced to a map with fewer countries by removing two boundaries as illustrated on the portion of the map shown below:

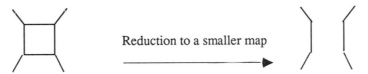

Reduction to a smaller map

The new map can be four coloured because it has fewer countries than any counterexample. This four colouring can then be used to four colour the original map.

The contradiction shows that the minimal counterexample contains **no** country adjacent to only four others.

Kempe went on to prove other results about the minimal counterexample, eventually showing that no such counterexample could exist. Unfortunately, there was an error in Kempe's proof.